ŚRĪ-ŚRĪ-DĀNA KELI CINTĀMAṆIḤ

Rādhā and Kṛṣṇa's Tax Game

Śrīla Raghunātha Dāsa Gosvāmī

With *bhāvārthānuvāda* of Śrīla Haridās dāsjī

Translation by Advaita dāsa

Copyright © 2000 by Rasbihari Lal & Sons
ISBN - 81-87812-07-9

Designed and Layout by Śrī Nitāi dāsa

Published by Rasbihari Lal & Sons
Loi Bazar, Vrindavan-281121 U.P INDIA
Phone: 0565-442570
Fax: 0565-443092
Our other division is Brijwasi Exports

Printed at:
Rakmo Press Pvt. Ltd., New Delhi-110 020.

Contents

PREFACE

Śrīla Haridās dāsjī (1898-1957) was one of the foremost Gauḍīya Vaiṣṇava saints, scholars, translators and publishers. He also compiled some books himself, namely Gauḍīya Vaiṣṇava Jīvana (a collection of biographies of all the important Gauḍīya Vaiṣṇava saints from the 15th to the 20th Century) and Gauḍīya Vaiṣṇava Abhidhāna (an encyclopaedia / lexicon for Gauḍīya Vaiṣṇavas). He took initiation from Harimohana Gosvāmī and ve a from Giridhāri Haribolā Bābājī. Many of his books are still available from Haribol Kutir (where he lived and worked on his books), Poḍā Ghāta, Navadvīpa. Full biographies of Śrīla Haridās Dāsjī can be found in the appendix of his 'Gauḍīya Vaiṣṇava Jīvana' (in Bengali) and in Dr. O.B.L. Kapoor's 'The Saints of Bengal' (in English).

LETTER OF DEDICATION

Parama Pūjyapāda —
ŚRĪ-ŚRĪ-YUKTA GOVINDA DĀSA BĀBĀJI

Mahānta Mahārājera Śrī-Śrī Kara-kamaleṣu —

Dearmost Govinda dādā,

When I considered the essence to be rejectable, being puffed up by Western education, I received a merciful indication from one of your dearmost servants and went to Śrī Haridāsa Ṭhākura's Maṭha in Purī Dhāma, where I was constantly showered by your causeless grace. Constantly hearing the nectarean topics of Śrī-Śrī Rādhā-Ramaṇa from your mouth, I became supremely satiated. The course of my life was reversed — although you knew how unqualified and insignificant I was you engaged me in the service of Śrī-Śrī Nitāi-Gaura-Sītānātha's lotusfeet and taught me the intricacies of each devotional service. You cast all the troubles that came with your own old age away and taught me devotional service — you were most happy to feed the *sādhus* and Vaiṣṇavas without even eating anything yourself and you embraced those who were rejected and despised by

society and gave them so much respect, love and affection. You were the friend of the fallen and the shelter of the homeless. Anyone who ever had your nectar-sweet association sings your glories with a loud voice — hence I say, O my *dādā* (elder brother)! Will you never teach me devotional service in Haridās Ṭhākura's Maṭha again by sweetly rebuking me? Will you never bless this unfortunate soul again by giving me your own bodily service? Alas! Will I never see you again in Śrīdhāma Navadvīpa, enjoying so many wonderful pastimes with your associates, eating with them, giving dust and rolling over until you fell into the Gangā? Will you never take this servant of your servants along anymore to *līlā*-places like Śrī Vṛndāvana, Śrī Nandagrāma and Barṣāṇā, making me relish the nectarean topics of Śrī-Śrī Rādhā Ramaṇa? Will this Dhūli-dāna-*līlā* and Khañjana Naṭana *līlā* and other most blissful pastimes performed during the Govardhana Parikramā, again cross the path of the eyes of this unfortunate soul? Will you never give me the service of sweeping the area around Śrī Rādhākuṇḍa with tear-filled eyes anymore, knowing that this service was very dear to Śrī Rādhā Ramaṇa? Dādā, this unfortunate soul was not able to follow any of your orders — he did not know how to love you even slightly — that is why, I understand, you have vanished from our eyes. Now you are relishing the *nitya līlā* with Śrī-Śrī Rādhā Ramaṇa, Śrīla Navadvīpa Dādā and their associates, but, O dādā, even now you have no peace, even now you seek the welfare of this unfortunate soul — even now you are broadcasting this transcendental message of love through your beloved devotees — you liked to see us as beggars, therefore one of your dear servants dressed your unfortunate soul as a beggar.

O beloved brother of mine! Your Haridāsa has found Parama Pūjyapāda Śrīmad Raghunātha dāsa Gosvāmī Mahodaya's wonderful composition *Dāna Keli Cintāmaṇi,* a jewel-like book, in Śrī Vṛndāvana — this unfortunate soul, who is blinded by illusion, has first offered this priceless scripture in the hands of your dear servant Śrī Giridhārījī — he has removed the dirt from this jewel in the shape of the different misplaced mistakes and has sent it to one of your dear younger sisters to have it strung into a beautiful garland; through her endeavours and eagerness Śrīla Narahari Sarakāra Ṭhākura's Vaṁśāvataṁsa (ornament of his dynasty) Śrīpāda Rākhālānanda Śāstrī and Śrī-Śrī Sītānātha Vaṁśa Bhūṣaṇa (ornament of Śrī Advaita Prabhu's dynasty) Śrī-yukta Ānanda Gopāla Gosvāmī Prabhupāda and others have offered their utmost assistance in making a nice garland of these Cintāmaṇis, in many different ways and with different meters and words — if you were still present in the manifest pastimes today, the heart of this unfortunate soul would be soothed as he could make you wear this nicely strung garland of Cintāmaṇis — anyhow, since your pastimes are true in all three phases of time (past, present and future), they are still going on now — hence I am offering this jewel-like book into your sacred lotus-hands — you will make all your dear associates like Śrī-Śrī Rādhā Ramaṇa, Śrīla Navadvīpa dādā and Śrī-yukta Mādhava dāsa Bābājī Mahārāja relish this and you will bless me that I will keep my head under your lotusfeet and I will sing your glories, so that I can keep the subject matter of this booklet within my heart. Iti —

Desiring your affection —
Hari dāsa

Foreword

Today the long-standing sacred desires of the devotee-readers have become fulfilled, for as a nectarean result of the collecting-work of Śrīmān Haridās dās Bābā the jewellike book named "Śrī Dāna Keli Cintāmaṇi", which was written by Śrīpāda Raghunātha dāsa Gosvāmī Mahodaya, who is one of the worshipable six Gosvāmīs, who is the sun of the devotees, and who is wholly absorbed in the nectartaste of Śrī Rādhā, has been published. By reading his preface, the readers can somewhat understand how much trouble, endeavour and work Śrīmān Bābājī Mahāśaya has gone through to publish this book. Those who do not accept household life and are engaged in *bhajana*, taking a vow of renunciation, and those among them who are well educated, are kindly following in the footsteps of the Gosvāmīs, and for the sake of the ordinary people collect these books, that bring human life to perfection by means of *prema bhakti*, then print them with word-for-word translation, commentaries and Bengali translation, are accomplishing their own welfare by performing their own *sādhana* by studying these *tattva* and *līlā*-books in the process, and at the same time they are rendering a greatly beneficial service to the people in general by teaching them these scriptures. Especially beneficial are those who save these books, that are about to go lost, from the destroying hands of time are saving the *kīrti-stambha* (monument) of the Mahājanas, leaving it unimpaired and well-established. It need not be told to anyone that studying and teaching the scriptures on *tattva* and *līlā* is counted as one of the main principles of *bhajana*. In this the limbs of *śravaṇa*, *kīrtana* and *smaraṇa* are contained in an excellent and relishable way that cannot be established through other means. In this connection Śrīpāda Śukadeva Gosvāmī said — "In this age of Kali, which is so full of obstacles, there is no other way to cross the ocean of material existence than to relish the flavours of the Lord's pastimes." Therefore, there is no doubt about it that the study of this class of books, that are the greatest aids to *bhajana*, is a form *bhajana* that causes tremendous happiness.

I have intensively studied each syllable of this sacred scripture and have become outright enchanted by it. By reading this book of Śrīpāda Dāsa Gosvāmī we can understand that due to the power of his language, his use of sweet and lovely words and easily understandable Sanskrit compounds, his glorious use of *alaṅkāras* (metaphors), both literally and figuratively, that are respectable by all *alaṅkārikas* (Sanskrit poets) in all respects, this Bhāṇikā (one-act play) deserves the highest ranking. On top of that, the zenith of Śrī-Śrī Yugala Kiśora's *madhura rasa vilāsa* — that *rasa,* which, according to the *alaṅkārikas,* is the very life-force of poetry, and the astonishment which is the essence of *rasa* — is shown in this Bhāṇikā. By reading this book we can perfectly see how much Śrīpāda Raghunātha dāsa Mahodaya attained the same *bhāva* as Śrīpāda Rūpa Gosvāmī Mahāśaya, as a result of following in his footsteps in the different aspects of his poetry. If this book had not been the signed and confirmed work of Śrīla Dāsa Gosvāmī, then nobody would have had any doubt that it was composed by Śrīla Rūpapāda in its entirety. This booklet is so sweet and so beautiful, and causes so much *rasika* astonishment and attraction within the hearts of the devotees that no one would grasp it through these insignifant words of mine without personally reading it.

The Bhāṇa-type of theatrical poetry is generally very relishable — When Śrīmad Raghunātha had read 'Lalita Mādhava' his heart became stirred with feelings of love-in-separation, so Śrīpāda Rūpa Gosvāmī Mahodaya wrote Dāna Keli Kaumudī to make his heart blossom with delight. As a result of swimming in this ocean of great *rasa* a great stream of *rasa* was created in Śrīmad Dāsa Gosvāmī's heart, that became externally manifest as this book. The two books "Dāna Keli Kaumudī" and 'Dāna Keli Cintāmaṇi" deal with the same topic and we are unable to pass a judgement on them or criticize them in any way, for both (Rūpa and Raghunātha) are *sampradāyācāryas,* both are the heart's friends of all the Vaiṣṇavas in the world and both are dishing out the brilliant and elevated flavours of transcendental Vraja. Indeed, they cannot be compared with anyone — I would consider it to be a great insult to compare these two books with each other in beauty and sweetness, in depth of feelings, in opulence of eloquence, in glory of emotion, or to say which of the two books is more charming and attractive and satisfying to the heart than the other. Hence I will not commence such a bold and unjust endeavour. I just like to submit at the gate of the hearts of the readers, that are filled with *prema bhakti rasa,* that those who have already read ''Dāna Keli Kaumudī' will once read this 'Dāna Keli Cintāmaṇi', that has been brought before our eyes by the grace of the Lord — they will see that as they are reading they will be merged within an ocean of transcendental bliss — they will give up all endeavours to criticise and will be immersed in relishing the nectar of Vraja-*rasa* after their hearts have been lifted into a most astonishing transcendental kingdom of bliss. In this book from the beginning — what are the ingredients of a Bhāṇikā, what is the elegance of a Bhāṇikā, what cleverness is used in the playful quarrels of a Bhāṇikā — the ascertainment of the tax with all its great sweetness, beauty and prowess, and the *rasa kandala* (tasty quarrel) that is performed by both parties to attain it — all this will give great ecstasy to the hearts of the devotees. The sights at Girirāja and the description of the forest around the banks of Mānasa Gaṅgā, that is caused and enhanced by its flowers and leaves, will also be very relishable to the poets. When the *premika bhakta*-readers are so fortunate to just once see the great beauty and sweetness of this transcendental kingdom they will be able to understand how utterly low the level of this material world is and how insignificant is its sense gratification. I had the desire to analyse the *rasa, bhāva,* sweetness and beauty of each and every topic, placing it before the eyes of my like-minded heart's friends, just for their relish, but to reveal these ecstasies that are *mūkāsvādanavat,* relishable for the dumb, through verbal expressions or through words is simply impossible. Especially since I am disabled due to old age and its many diseases it will not be possible for me to do so in this birth. Therefore I just revealed my humble opinion with my heart's desire for the welfare of Bābājī Mahāśaya, who is the object of my great love and affection. I hope that the merciful readers will be intoxicated by relishing the nectar-flavours of this book and that the great work, worries and endeavours of the publisher in accomplishing the word-for-word translation of the Sanskrit text and the flowing Bengali translation will result in the endless blessings of the Lord's lotusfeet.

Śrī Rasika Mohana Deva Śarmā Vidyābhūṣaṇa
25, Bāg Bazar Street, Calcutta
15th Āśvina — 451 Gaurābda
(October 1937)

Introduction

The author of this jewellike book named *Śrī Dāna Keli Cintāmaṇi* is Śrīpāda Raghunātha dāsa Gosvāmī Mahodaya. It is no exaggaration to say that he needs no introduction to the Gauḍīya Vaiṣṇava world — he who, in his adolescence, gave up wealth equal to that of Indra and a wife as beautiful as an Apsarā, ignoring all the pleas and endeavours of his father and mother to keep him at home, he who, maddened by the love of Śrīman Mahāprabhu, gave up his home and went to Nīlācala (Jagannātha Puri) to meet the Lord, he who, for sixteen years, practised harsh dispassion and thus attained the eligibility for Śrīman Mahāprabhu's intimate service along with Śrīpāda Svarūpa Dāmodara, he who was blessed by Śrīman Mahāprabhu by receiving a Guñjā-*mālā* and a Govardhana Śilā from Him, he who came to Vṛndāvana, vowing to commit suicide by jumping from Govardhana Hill out of separation from Śrīman Mahāprabhu, he who was showered by the ambrosial grace of Śrī-Śrī Rūpa-Sanātana and thus spent twenty-four hours a day in the glorification of Rādhā and Giridhārī on the bank of Rādhākuṇḍa in perfect renunciation — who has not heard of that Raghunātha dāsa Gosvāmī Mahodaya?

Śrīpāda Raghunātha dāsa Gosvāmī has composed three jewel-like books. They are revealed in *Bhakti Ratnākara*:

raghunātha dāsa gosvāmī grantha-traya;
stavamālā nāma stavāvalī yāre koy
śrī dāna carita muktā carita madhura
yāhāra śravaṇe mahā-duḥka yāya dūra
tathā hi—
raghunāthābhidheyasya tayor mitratvam īyuṣaḥ
stavamālā dāna muktā caritaṁ kṛtisūditam

"Raghunātha Dāsa Gosvāmī, who was the friend of both Rūpa and Sanātana Gosvāmī, has written three books — Stavamālā, which is now called Stavāvalī, Śrī Dāna Carita (Dāna Keli Cintāmaṇi) and Muktā Carita. When one hears these sweet books even the greatest suffering goes far away."

Descriptions of Śrī Kṛṣṇa-*līlā* and Vraja-*dhāma* are the main features of 'Stavāvalī', and 'Muktā Carita' deals with Śrī Rādhā and Mādhava's playful loving quarrel over the purchase and sale of pearls. These books have been published before, but this Dāna Carita or Dāna Keli Cintāmaṇi[*] has remained hidden from the people's eyes so far — now, by the grace of Śrīpāda Dāsa Gosvāmī, it has been printed.

This book was probably written between 1550 and 1554, because Śrīla Raghunātha composed it after Śrīpāda Rūpa Gosvāmī composed his 'Dāna Keli Kaumudī'. 'Dāna Keli Kaumudī' was written in 1550 (1471 Śaka era)[1], therefore it would not have taken more than three or four years to make this book (Dāna Keli Cintāmaṇi)[2].

---

[*] There is no doubt about it that the 'Dāna Carita' mentioned in Bhakti Ratnākara and 'Dāna Keli Cintāmaṇi' are the same book. In the Catalog of Theodor Aufrecht's Catalogus Catalogorum it is also mentioned as 'Dāna Keli Cintāmaṇi'. "Dāna Keli Cintāmaṇi — a poem, describing the dalliance between Radha and Krishna".

After composing his 'Lalita Mādhava Nāṭaka' Śrīmad Rūpa Gosvāmī-caraṇa read the book to Śrīpāda Raghunātha. When Śrīla Raghunātha read this book he plunged into an ocean of *viraha* and became as if mad. Sometimes he held the jewel-like book to his chest and showered the surface of the earth with his tears, and sometimes he would cry out "Hā Rādhe! Prāṇeśvari!!" and fall into a swoon, becoming motionless. It goes without saying that, although Śrīpāda Dāsa Gosvāmī was always very close to Śrīmatī on the bank of Śrī Rādhākuṇḍa, he would be very unsteady and agitated whenever he felt separation from Her for even a moment. On top of that, the course of events described in Lalita Mādhava thrust Dāsa Gosvāmī in an ocean of *viraha*, making it hard for him to remain alive. When Śrīla Rūpa Gosvāmī heard about this loving distress, agitation and madness of Śrīmad Raghunātha he composed a jewel-like book named Śrī Dāna Keli Kaumudī, that was filled with eternal *sambhoga* (the *rasa* of union), laughter and joking, and had it sent to Dāsa Gosvāmī, taking the Lalita Mādhava back from him on the pretext of wanting to edit it. Śrī Dāsa Gosvāmī's mind thus entered into another *rasa* and he became somewhat calm, so that he was able to compose the two incomparible, jewel-like books named 'Muktā Carita' and 'Dāna Keli Cintāmaṇi', that are filled with the sweet *sambhoga rasa*. Śrīmad Rūpa Gosvāmī has repeatedly mentioned Śrī Raghunātha in his 'Dāna Keli Kaumudī', for instance 1) in the *prastāvanā* (commencement of the play) — *yad eṣa niyogena suhṛdām uparūpak-abhidāṁ dāna keli kaumudīṁ nāma bhāṇikām abhinetum udyato'smi* — "I have commenced this one-act play named

---

[1] *ate manuśate śāke candra svara samanvite; nandīśvare nivasato bhāṇikeyaṁ vinirmitā* "I composed this Bhāṇika (one-act play) Dāna Keli Kaumudi in the year 1471 Śaka era while residing in Nandīśvara (Nandagrāma). (Dāna Keli Kaumudi pariśiṣṭa)

[2] It is also widely accepted that Śrīla Rūpa Gosvāmī left this world in 1554. Ed.

Dāna Keli Kaumudī after receiving the consent of my heart's friends (to give them loving pleasure)."

2) In the Bharata-vākya- (towards the end of the book)

rādhākuṇḍa taṭī kuṭīra vasatis tyaktānya karma janaḥ
sevām eva samakṣam atra yuvayor yaḥ kartum utkaṇṭhate
vṛndāraṇya samṛddhi dohada pada krīḍā kaṭākṣa dyute
tarṣākhyā tarur asya mādhava
phalī tūrṇaṁ vidheyas tvayā

"O Mādhava! My friend (Raghunātha Dāsa) has given up all other activities and is now living in a cottage on the bank of Rādhākuṇḍa, very anxious to exclusively serve You and Śrī Rādhikā. You always cast Your merciful glance on those who live in Vṛndāvana and You fulfill all their desires, so please make the tree of his (Raghunātha's) aspirations bear fruit soon!"

3) At the end of the book —

grathitā sumanaḥ sukhadā
yasya nideśena bhāṇikā srag iyam
tasya mama priya suhṛdaḥ
kuṇḍa-taṭīṁ kṣaṇam alaṅkurutām

"On the request of my dearest heart's friend (Śrīla Raghunātha Dāsa Gosvāmī) I have composed this one-act play, as if stringing a garland of delightful flowers. May this momentarily decorate the bank of the (Rādhā) *kuṇḍa*."

In this book Śrī Rādhā-Govinda's *naimittika* (occasional) Dāna-*līlā* is described. The hearer is Kundalatā, the wife of Upananda's son Subhadra, and the speaker is her girlfriend Sumukhī. At Govinda Kuṇḍa, a lake at the base of

Govardhana Giri, Maharṣi Bhāgurī is performing a *yajña* and Śrī Rādhā and the *gopīs* depart from the bank of Rādhākuṇḍa to bring fresh *ghī* to that sacrifice, carrying it on their heads. Śrī Kṛṣṇa stands near a self-erected toll-station on top of Girirāja, surrounded by His friends. When Nāgara and Nāgarī see Each other, They drink the sweetness of Each other's beautiful forms. On Madhumaṅgala's indication Śrī Kṛṣṇa and His friends block the path of Śrī Rādhā and Her girlfriends, and a verbal quarrel ensues, in which each of Śrī Rādhārāṇī's limbs is described in a joking manner on the pretext of levying tax, and Kṛṣṇa prays to Her for enjoyment of each of these particular limbs. When this dispute reaches its climax and the Vraja-sundarīs take the pots with *ghī* from their heads, remaining on the base of Girirāja, suddenly Nāndīmukhī appears on the scene. Even in front of her, Śrī Kṛṣṇa extends His *rasika* naughtiness and Śrī Rādhā pierces Śyāmasundara with the arrows of Her glances, feigning anger. Nāndīmukhī then pacifies both parties with different consoling words. After the Yugala Kiśora enjoy the bliss of meeting in a solitary cave of Govardhana Hill Śrī Kṛṣṇa returns to His duty of herding His cows, while Śrī Rādhā and Her friends proceed to the sacrificial arena at Govinda Kuṇḍa. Even then both parties experience great bliss in discussing this pleasant Dāna-*līlā* with Each other.

Śrī Dāsa Gosvāmī has personally acknowledged that this book is the fruit of Śrīpāda Rūpa Gosvāmī's mercy (see verses 174 and 175) and he became blessed by offering many bouquets of flowers in the form of humble words of praise at the beautiful lotus-foot-soles of Śrī Rūpa. Factually this Dāna Keli Cintāmaṇi is as wonderfully relishable as Śrī Dāna Keli Kaumudī is. In two ways these two authors have relished the blissful story of the Dāna-*līlā* and have presented it to the devotees accordingly. May the *rasi-*

ka devotees that follow Śrīpāda Rūpa Gosvāmī be blessed by chewing his remnants!

Finally a few more words must be dedicated to the attainment and the printing of this booklet. I first found this book with Śrī Vṛndāvana's Śrī-yukta Vanamālī-lāl Gosvāmī Mahāśaya, but there were many mistakes in this version. After this, Śrī-yukta Rādhā-Caraṇa dāsa Bābājī Mahārāja found me another version of this book — in this version were also a lot of mistakes. After this I received a copy from Barāhanagara's Pāṭa-bāḍī's Grantha Mandira — here were also mistakes. Śrī-yukta Rākhālānanda Ṭhākura Śāstrī, the scholar of innumerable books, was so kind to edit this book from the root (the original Sanskrit text, ed.), despite his different physical inconveniences, and offered a lot of assistance on the *anvaya* (word-for-word translation). Śrī-yukta Ānanda Gopāla Gosvāmī Mahāśaya and Śrīla Yadu-Gopāla Gosvāmī were amongst those who greatly assisted me in relishing the *bhāva-mādhurya* (the sweetness of the feelings expressed in the book, ed.), and finally Vaiṣṇavācārya-vara Śrī-yukta Rasika Mohana Vidyābhūṣaṇa Mahāśaya was so kind to write an introduction and bless this fallen servant by assisting him with so many kinds of advice. This book was printed due to the graceful order and the eagerness of Śrī-yukta Dīneśa-caraṇa dāsa Dādā Mahāśaya and through the financial help of some *sāhityānurāgī bhaktas* (devotees who love transcendental literature). This fallen servant acknowledges deep devotional gratitude to the lotusfeet of all these devotees. Factually, if I had not received their merciful help I could never have mustered the courage to engage in this work. Although so much effort was made, printing mistakes could not be altogether avoided. I hope that the readers will forgive me for any accidental mistake. O sensitive readers! Since you are completely free from the propensity of fault-finding, please ignore all the faults a fallen soul like me, who is a complete baby in Vaiṣṇava-*śāstras* and is completely ignorant of *rasa siddhānta,* and may you attain the topmost transcendental bliss in gauging the deep purports of the original text of this book — this is my prayer.

Śrī Haridās dāsa Vaiṣṇava Dāsānudāsa
Śrī Haribol Kuṭīra
Śrīdāma Navadvīpa
Āśvina — 451 Caitanyābda (October, 1937)

Śrī Dāna Keli Cintāmaṇi

kurvānaiḥ śatam āśiṣam
nija nija preyo jayāyo sukaiḥ
svīya svīya gaṇaiḥ sphuṭam kuṭilayā vācāti tuṅgīkṛtaḥ
gavyānāṁ nava dāna kalpana
kṛte prauḍham mithaḥ spardhinor
gāndharvā giridhārinor giritaṭe keli kaliḥ pātu vaḥ

kurvānaiḥ - granting; *śatam* - hundreds; *āśiṣam* - blessings; *nija nija* - their own; *preyaḥ* - beloved; *jayāya* - for victory; *utsukaiḥ* - by those who are eager; *svīya svīya* - by their own; *gaṇaiḥ* - parties; *sphuṭam* - clearly; *kuṭilayā* - by the crooked; *vāca* - words; *ati tuṅgīkṛtaḥ* - by the elevated; *gavyānāṁ* - of milk products; *nava* - new; *dāna* - gift; *kalpana kṛte* - in the consideration; *prauḍham* - increased; *mithaḥ* - mutually; *spardhinoḥ* - of the two challengers; *gāndharvā giridhārinoḥ* - of Rādhā and Kṛṣṇa; *giritaṭe* - at the base of the hill; *keli* - play; *kaliḥ* - quarrel; *pātu* - may protect; *vaḥ* - you.

May the playful quarrel of Śrī-Śrī Gāndharvā-Giridhārī (Rādhā-Kṛṣṇa) about the tax on *ghī* at the base of Govardhana Hill, in which They challenge Each other with the help of the crooked, insinuating words of Their hundreds of supporters (cowherd

boys- and girls), that were eager for their parties' victory, protect you all! (1)

Notes: *keli kalir ityanena vastu nirdeśaḥ pātviti karṇa-caṣakeṇa pāyayitvā tad rasāviṣṭaṁ karotvityāśīrvādaś ca vyañjitaḥ* "By pointing out the topic as a 'playful quarrel', and saying 'may this protect you', the author offers this blessing— "May you become absorbed in this *rasa* by drinking it through the cups of your ears!"

uddāma narma rasa-raṅga taraṅga kānta
rādhā sarid giridharārṇava saṅgamottham
śrī rūpa cāru caraṇābja rajaḥ prabhāvād
andho'pi dāna nava keli maṇiṁ cinomi

uddāma - exalted; *narma* - humorous; *rasa-raṅga* - *rasika* fun; *taraṅga* - waves; *kānta* - beautiful; *rādhā sarid* - the Rādhā-river; *giridharārṇava* - the Giridhārī-ocean; *saṅgama* - meeting; *uttham* - arisen; *śrī rūpa* - Śrīla Rūpa Gosvāmī; *cāru* - beautiful; *caraṇābja* - lotusfeet; *rajaḥ* - dust; *prabhāvād* - on the strength; *andha* - blind; *api* - even; *dāna* - gift; *nava* - new; *keli* - play; *maṇiṁ* - jewel; *cinomi* - picking.

Although I am blind I picked up the new Cintāmaṇi-gem of the Dāna Keli by the power of (my service to) Śrīla Rūpa Gosvāmī's beautiful foot dust. This jewel sprang forth from the meeting of the Rādhā-river with the Giridhārī-ocean, which is full of high waves of humorous sportive activities!" (2)

Notes: *cayanaṁ kṛtvā kuṇḍalaṁ karomi yena śrotra-parisara-maṇḍanaṁ suṣṭhu sampatsyatetarām iti bhāvaḥ. atra 'caraṇābja-rajaḥ' ityanena sundara sugandhi rasamaya bhakti-janakatvaṁ parāgasya jñāpatye, tathā* *citta-rūpa-darpaṇasya malāpasaraṇa-kāritvaṁ sundara nayanāmṛtāñjanam ivājñāna timira-nāśa-pūrvaka śrī rādhā-govinda raho-līlā prakāśatvaṁ ca vyajyate*

"I collected this Cintāmaṇi gem to make earrings with which you can nicely decorate your ears (by hearing this narration). The foot-dust mentioned here is beautiful, fragrant and tasty lotus pollen which generates devotion. This dust removes the dirt from the mirror of the heart and acts like a beautiful, nectarean eye-ointment that destroys the darkness of ignorance and reveals the intimate pastimes of Śrī Rādhā-Govinda."

sāhārākhyaṁ jayati sadanaṁ gokule gokuleśa
bhrātā mantrī vasati sumatis tatra nāmnopanandaḥ
tasya śrīman nikhila guṇavān sūnur adya subhadro
bhāryā tasyātula kulavatī kunda pūrva latā'ste

sāhara - Sāhara; *akhyaṁ* - renowned; *jayati* - all glories to; *sadanaṁ* - the abode; *gokule* - in Gokula; *goku-la-īśa* - the Lord of Gokula, Nanda; *bhrātā* - brother; *mantrī* - counsellor; *vasati* - abode; *sumatiḥ* - intelligent, wise; *tatra* - there; *nāmna* - with the name; *upanandaḥ* - Upānanda; *tasya* - his; *śrīman* - beautiful, opulent; *nikhila* - all; *guṇavān* - qualified; *sūnuḥ* - the son; *adya* - own; *sub-hadraḥ* - Subhadra; *bhāryā* - wife; *tasya* - his; *atula* - matchless; *kulavatī* - housewife; *kunda pūrva latā* - named Kundalatā; *aste* - is.

All glories to the village named Sāhāra in Gokula, where Nanda Mahārāja's intelligent brother and counsellor Upānanda lives. His oldest son, who is adorned with all good qualities, is named Subhadra, and Subhadra's matchless wife is named Kundalatā. (3)

puṣpair bhṛṅgair vividha vihagair bhrājad ūrvīruhānāṁ
ṣaṇḍaiḥ samyag vilasitatame niṣkuṭe saurabhāḍhye
khelantyoru praṇayam anayā hanta kutrādhunā tau
kurvate kiṁ kim iti sumukhī tatra pṛṣṭā vayasyā

puṣpaiḥ - by flowers; *bhṛṅgaiḥ* - by bees; *vividha* - different kinds; *vihagaiḥ* - by birds; *bhrājad* - shining; *ūrvīruhānāṁ* - by trees; *ṣaṇḍaiḥ* - by multitudes; *samyak* - completely; *vilasitatame* -beautified; *niṣkuṭe* - in a sub-forest; *saurabha* - fragrance; *aḍhye* - in the opulence; *khelantya* - playing; *uru* - great; *praṇayam* - love; *anayā* - with her; *hanta* - Aha!; *kutra* - where?; *adhunā* - now; *tau* - they; *kurvate* - doing; *kiṁ kim* - what; *iti* - thus; *sumukhī* - Sumukhī; *tatra* - there; *pṛṣṭā* - question; *vayasyā* - girlfriend.

Close to Kundalatā's house is a fragrant garden with blissful trees that are full of flowers, bees and birds. While Kundalatā lovingly played there, she asked her friend Sumukhī: "O *sakhī*! Where are Rādhā and Kṛṣṇa, and what are They doing now?" (4)

tasyāḥ śrīmad vadana kamalāj jalpa mādhvīka dhārā-
syandam rādhā girivaradhara praśna karpūra kamram
pītvānandocchalita pulakojjṛmbha sambhāvuka śrīḥ
sa tad vārtāṁ prathayitum athārambham utkā cakāra

śastasyārthe sva suta halino mitra putrāghaśatror
apy āsaktyā prati-nidhitayā śauriṇā sanniyuktaḥ
satraṁ kartuṁ rahasi bhagavān bhāgurir dīkṣato'bhūt
snehollāsaiḥ saha muni-gaṇas tatra govinda kuṇḍe

tasyāḥ - her; *śrīmad* - beautiful; *vadana* - face; *kamalāt* - from the lotus; *jalpa* - talks; *mādhvīka* - honey; *dhārā* - stream; *syandam* - trickling; *rādhā girivaradhara* -

Rādhā and Girivara-dhārī; *praśna* - questions; *karpūra* - camphor; *kamram* - lovely; *pītvā* - having drunk; *ānanda* - bliss; *ucchalita* - emanating; *pulaka* - goosepimples; *ujjṛmbha* - manifesting; *sambhāvuka śrīḥ* - complete beauty; *sa* - he; *tat* - of Them; *vārtām* - the news; *prathayitum* - extending; *atha* - then; *ārambham* - beginning; *utkā* - eager; *cakāra* - doing. *śastasya* - of auspiciousness; *arthe* - for the sake of; *sva* - his own; *suta* - son; *halinaḥ* - of Balarāma; *mitra* - friend; *putra* - son; *aghaśatroḥ* - of Kṛṣṇa; *api* - even; *āsaktyā* - through attachment; *pratinidhitayā* - as a substitute; *śauriṇā* - by Vasudeva; *sanniyuktaḥ* -engaged; *satram* - sacrifice; *kartum* - performing; *rahasi* - in secret; *bhagavān* - the noble; *bhāguriḥ* - Bhāgurī Muni; *dīkṣataḥ* - initiated; *abhūt* - became; *snehollāsaiḥ* - with affection and joy; *saha* - with; *muni-gaṇaḥ* - the great sages; *tatra* - there; *govinda kuṇḍe* - at Govinda Kuṇḍa.

Drinking these camphor-scented, honey-stream-like enquiries about Rādhā and Giridhārī that flowed from Kundalatā's beautiful lotus-like mouth, Sumukhī erupted with goosepimples of ecstasy and her bodily luster increased as she enthusiastically replied: "For the welfare of his son Balarāma and for the son of his friend, Śrī Kṛṣṇa, Vasudeva engaged Bhāgurī Muni in a sacrifice in solitude, so in great loving ecstasy that great sage went to Govinda Kuṇḍa (a tank that lies a little beyond the village of Anyora at the base of Govardhana Hill) with other *munis* to perform this sacrifice." (5-6)

tasmin satre ruciram aciram navya gavyam svayam yā
dhṛtvā nītam śirasi śucayo dadyur ābhīra vāmāḥ
tābhyaḥ kāmān atha maṇi-gaṇālaṅkṛtiḥ saubhagam ca
prītyā satyam sadasi munayo hanta yacchanti sadyaḥ

tasmin - in that; *satre* - in the sacrifice; *ruciram* - enchanting; *aciram* - quickly; *navya* - fresh; *gavyaṁ* - dairy products; *svayam* - personally; *yā* - who; *dhṛtvā* - having carried; *nītam* - taken; *śirasi* -on the head; *śucayaḥ* - pure; *dadyuḥ* - gave; *ābhīra vāmāḥ* - beautiful *gopīs*; *tābhyaḥ* - to them; *kāmān* - desires; *atha* - and; *maṇi-gaṇa* - gems; *ālaṅkṛtiḥ* - decoration; *saubhagaṁ* - auspiciousness; *ca* - and; *prītyā* - with love; *satyam* - in truth; *sadasi* - in the assembly; *munayaḥ* - sages; *hanta* - aha!; *yacchanti* - offer; *sadyaḥ* - at once.

"With love these sages gave valuable rewards like jewelled ornaments and blessings to any pure-hearted *gopī* who swiftly brought the required amount of milk products to this sacrifice, personally carrying it on their heads in pitchers". (7)

nānā vṛkṣair madhukara ruta syandi puṣpābhiramyaiḥ
kuñja stomair api ca paritas tādṛśair bhrājitasya
saurabhyāḍhyaiḥ kumuda kamalaiḥ sādhu phullair virājat
pānīyasya sva kṛta sarasas tīra kuñje vasantī

śrutvaivaitan nibhṛta vivṛtiṁ sūkṣmadhī śārikāsyād
utkaṇṭhābhis taralita manāḥ sa priyāligaṇā sā
snatvā samyag vividha vasanair bhūṣaṇair bhūṣitā drāk
kāśmīrais tat praṇaya paṭalair apy alaṁ rūṣitā ca

kṛtvā pūjām atha dina-pateḥ śuddha bhāvena śuddhā
baddhākāṅkṣaṁ hṛdaya gagane goṣṭha-candraṁ smarantī
haimaṁ kumbhaṁ nihita vikasad gandha haiyāṅgavīnaṁ
dhṛtvā prītyā śirasi calitā rādhikā svīya kuṇḍāt

nānā - different; *vṛkṣaiḥ* - by trees; *madhukara* - bumblebees; *ruta* - sounds; *syandi* - streaming; *puṣpa* - flowers; *abhiramyaiḥ* - charming; *kuñja* - bower; *stomaiḥ* -

by multitudes *api* - even; *ca* - and; *paritaḥ* - all around; *tādṛśaiḥ* - by the similar; *bhrājitasya* - of the shining; *saurabhya* - with a fragrance; *aḍhyaiḥ* - enriched; *kumuda* - lilies; *kamalaiḥ* - by lotusflowers; *sādhu* - nice; *phullaiḥ* - with blossoms; *virājat* - splendid; *pānīyasya* - of the drinking-water; *sva* - own; *kṛta* - done; *sarasaḥ* - lake; *tīra* - bank; *kuñje* - in the grove; *vasantī* - they reside. *śrutvā* - having heard; *eva* - certainly; *etad* - this; *nibhṛta* - in solitude; *vivṛtiṁ* - revealed; *sūkṣmadhī* - Sūkṣmadhī; *śārika* - female parrot; *asyād* - from her mouth; *utkaṇṭhābhiḥ* - with eagerness; *taralita* - agitated; *manāḥ* - mind; *sa* - with; *priya* - dear; *aligaṇā* - girlfriends; *sā* - she; *snatvā* - having bathed; *samyak* - completely; *vividha* - different kinds; *vasanaiḥ* - by garments; *bhūṣaṇaiḥ* - with ornaments; *bhūṣitā* - decorated; *drāk* - at once; *kāśmīraiḥ* - with vermilion; *tat* - Their; *praṇaya paṭalaiḥ* - with a lot of love; *api* - even; *alaṁ* - grealy; *rūṣitā* - anointed; *ca* - and. *kṛtvā* - having done; *pūjām* - the worship; *atha* - and; *dina-pateḥ* - of the sun; *śuddha* - pure; *bhāvena* - with feeling; *śuddhā* - pure; *baddha* - binding; *ākāṅkṣaṁ* - desire; *hṛdaya* - heart; *gagane* - in the sky; *goṣṭha-candraṁ* - the moon of the meadows; *smarantī* - they remember; *haimaṁ* - golden; *kumbhaṁ* - jugs; *nihita* - placing; *vikasad* - manifesting; *gandha* - scent; *haiyāṅgavīnaṁ* - with fresh *ghī; dhṛtvā* - holding; *prītyā* - with love; *śirasi* - on the head; *calitā* - went; *rādhikā* - Rādhikā; *svīya* - own; *kuṇḍāt* - from the pond.

At that time Śrī Rādhikā stayed in one of Her *kuñjas* on the bank of Her lake (Rādhākuṇḍa), which was adorned with various beautiful trees that were full of honey-oozing flowers and humming bumblebees. The water of this lake was beautifully filled with fragrant blooming lotusflowers and lilies. When Śrī Rādhikā and Her girlfriends heard about the solitary sacrifice from a

female parrot named Sūksmadhī, their minds were stirred with eagerness. After a quick bath they dressed and ornamented themselves and anointed their bodies with vermilion and lots of love for their Priyatama (beloved Krsna). Then they finished their ritual worship of the Sungod with pure hearts and set out from Rādhākunda, lovingly putting golden pots with fresh *ghī* on their heads and remembering Krsna, the moon of Vraja, in their sky-like hearts that were filled with desire. (8-10)

Notes: *pūrvāhna eva dāna-līlā prasangah syād ity-atraisā mahājanānumodita prathā'nusartavyā. kadācid ravi-vāsare arunodaye brāhmana-mukhāc chruta yajña-vrttāntā jaratī pūrvāhna vyāpinyām śuklā saptamyām eva sūrya-pūjām avaśya kartavyatvena nirnīya yajña-bhavane ghrta-dānam api sva mangala nimittikam iti ca buddhā śrī rādhāyāh nandālaya-gamanam varjayitvādistavatī - 'he kalyāni! adya pūrvāhna-madhya eva sūrya-kundam gatvā snātānuliptā bhāskaram arcayitvā jhatiti yajña-bhavanam gaccheti'. tena ca śrī rādhāyāh nandālaya gostha-gamanādi prasānge śrī śyāmasundarasya darśanābhāve jāte mahotkanthitā sā śrī rādhākundam gatvaiva sthitā, tadaiva śārikā-mukhāt śruta krsna vrttāntā āśvastā satī snāna pūjādikam drutam samācarya govinda kundābhimukham caliteti sarvam samañjasam* — The Mahājanas (great devotional authorities) say that the Dāna-*līlā* takes place in the Pūrvāhna-time of the day (the forenoon, from 8.24 to 10.48 a.m.) and this must be followed. Once, at sunrise on a Sunday, Jatilā heard from a *brāhmana* that in the *pūrvāhna*-time, on the seventh day of the bright lunar fortnight, Sūrya Pūjā must certainly be done, and it is also very auspicious for Her to donate *ghī* to the sacrificial arena. Understanding this, she stopped Śrī Rādhā from going to Nandagrāma for Her usual cooking for

Kṛṣṇa, and said: "O Kalyāṇi (auspicious girl)! Today You must go to Sūrya-kuṇḍa in the *pūrvāhna*-time and, after bathing and anointing Yourself, worship the Sun. Then, after that, You must quickly proceed to the sacrificial abode!" Thus Śrī Rādhā was unable to see Śrī Śyāmasundara in Nandagrāma, or to see Him going to the *goṣṭha* afterwards. Thus filled with anxiety, She went to Śrī Rādhākuṇḍa, where She heard the latest news about Kṛṣṇa from the mouth of a Śārikā (female parrot). This pacified Her slightly and after finishing Her bath and *pūjā* there She quickly proceeded to Govinda Kuṇḍa...

smitvā smitvā pathi pathi mithaḥ kurvati kṛṣṇa-vārtām
ārtā tasyānavakalanataḥ snigdhatā śalabhañjī
prema stomollalita lalitāṁ narma phullad viśākhāṁ
dṛṣṭvā dṛṣṭvā sudati mumude narma-bhaṅgyā nikāmam

smitvā smitvā - smiling again and again; *pathi pathi* - on each path; *mithaḥ* - mutually; *kurvati* - speaking; *kṛṣṇa-vārtām* - news of Kṛṣṇa; *ārtā* - distressed; *tasya* - His; *anavakalanataḥ* - from not seeing; *snigdhatā* - affection; *śalabhañjī* - puppet; *prema* - love; *stoma* - abundance; *ullalita* - manifested; *lalitāṁ* - Lalitā; *narma* - humour; *phullad* - blossoming; *viśākhāṁ* - Viśākhāṁ; *dṛṣṭvā dṛṣṭvā* - constantly seeing; *sudati* - Kundalatā; *mumude* - blissful; *narma-bhaṅgyā* - joking gestures; *nikāmam* - constantly.

"O Sudati (Kundalate)! While walking down the road, Śrī Rādhikā, who is like a doll of affection, smiled again and again and eagerly spoke about Kṛṣṇa with Her girlfriends. Although She greatly suffered the pangs of separation from Kṛṣṇa She was very happy to see blissful Lalitā and Viśākhā, who blossomed with her humorous words and relished their blissful, joking words. (11)

*gandhair bhrājat kusuma paṭalī mṛṣṭa mādhvīka mādyad
bhrāmyad bhṛṅga prakara vilasac
chākha śākhi prapañcāḥ
śaspaiḥ sāndraiḥ subalita bhuvaḥ svādu sat kanda mūlā
nyañcad dhvāna dvija mṛga gaṇāś cāru nānā phalāni*

*sthāne sthāne vividha viṭapi kroḍha ratnoru vedyaḥ
sthāne sthāne parimala balad ratna siṁhāsanaughaḥ
sthāne sthāne vara jhara darī sānavo bhānti yasmin
śailendraṁ sa giridhara kara prāptamānaṁ dadarśa*

gandhaiḥ - with odours; *bhrājat* - shining; *kusuma paṭalī* - with flowers; *mṛṣṭa* - rubbed; *mādhvīka* - honey; *mādyad* - intoxicated; *bhrāmyad* - wandering; *bhṛṅga prakara* - bees; *vilasat* -shining; *śākha* - branches; *śākhi* - trees; *prapañcāḥ* - manifestation; *śaspaiḥ* - with grass; *sāndraiḥ* - with density; *subalita* - endowed; *bhuvaḥ* - earth; *svādu* - palatable; *sat* - nice; *kanda* - bulbs; *mūlāni* - roots; *añcad* - enchanting; *dhvāna* - sounds; *dvija* - birds; *mṛga-gaṇāḥ* - deer; *cāru* - lovely; *nānā* - different; *phalāni* - fruits. *sthāne sthāne* - in different places; *vividha* - various kinds; *viṭapi* - trees; *kroḍa* - roots; *ratna* - jewelled; *uru* - big; *vedyaḥ* - platforms; *sthāne sthāne* - at various places; *parimala* - fragrance; *balad* - manifesting; *ratna* - jewelled; *siṁhāsana* - lion-throne; *oghaḥ* - multitudes; *sthāne sthāne* - in various places; *vara* - excellent; *jhara* - cascades; *darī* - caves; *sānavaḥ* -valleys; *bhānti* - shining; *yasmin* - where-in; *śaila* - mountain; *indraṁ* - king; *sa* - him; *giridhara kara* - Giridhārī's hand; *prāptamānaṁ* - attaining; *dadarśa* - saw.

She saw the king of mountains proud of the touch of Giridhārī's hand, with its many beautiful trees with fragrant flowers on their branches that are surrounded by bees that zoom here and there, drunk from drinking their pure honey. The ground of Govardhana Hill is cov-

ered with luxuriant grass with sweet delicious roots, the birds and animals make sweet sounds and there are many kinds of delicious fruits everwhere. At the foot of the trees there are many jewelled platforms with fragrant jewelled thrones, beautiful streams, caves and valleys. (12- 13)

labdhvā govardhana girim atha prāpya saurabhya sāraṁ
śaśvat prītyā muni-vara gaṇair datta gavyā hutīnām
ākṛṣṭodyat sukha-bhara rasenāśu gantuṁ samutkā
sthūla śroṇī kuca-yuga-bharān mantharā tan nininda

labdhvā - having attained; *govardhana girim* - Govardhana Hill; *atha* - then; *prāpya* - attaining; *saurabhya* - fragrance; *sāraṁ* - essence; *śaśvat* - constantly; *prītyā* - with love; *muni-vara gaṇaiḥ* - by the group of the best sages; *datta* - given; *gavya* - of *ghī; ahutīnām* - of oblations; *ākṛṣṭa* - attracted; *udyat* - rising; *sukha-bhara* - great happiness; *rasena* - with taste; *āśu* - quickly; *gantuṁ* - going; *samutkā* - eager; *sthūla* - large; *śroṇī* - hips; *kuca* - breasts; *yuga* - of the pair; *bharāt* - because of the weight; *mantharā* - slowly; *tat* - them; *nininda* - criticized.

Reaching Govardhana Hill, Śrī Rādhikā was very happy to smell the fragrant *ghī* the sages were constantly offering to the sacrificial fire with great love, She became more and more ecstatic, and She rebuked Her breasts and buttocks, since She could not move fast enough because of their weight, although She was so eager to do so. (14)

jñatvā tāsāṁ gamanam aciraṁ kīra varyasya vaktrād
smitvā narma priya sakha-gaṇair āvṛtaḥ sāvadhānaḥ
śailendrasyopari parilasann udbhaṭa śyāma-vedyāṁ
ghaṭṭīpaṭṭaṁ vidadhad atulaṁ ballabādhīśa sūnuḥ

jñatvā -having learnt; *tāsāṁ* - of the girls; *gamanam* - going; *aciraṁ* - swiftly; *kīra* - parrot; *varyasya* - of the best; *vaktrāt* - from the mouth; *smitvā* - having smiled; *narma* - humorous; *priya* -dear; *sakha-gaṇaiḥ* - by the friends; *āvṛtaḥ* - surrounded; *sāvadhānaḥ* - carefully; *śailendrasya* - of the king of mountain; *upari* - above; *par-ilasann* - shining; *udbhaṭa* - raised; *śyāma-vedyāṁ* - on a black platform; *ghaṭṭī-paṭṭaṁ* - toll station; *vidadhad* - mak-ing; *atulaṁ* - unrivalled; *ballaba* - cowherds; *adhīśa* - the king; *sūnuḥ* - the son.

When Kṛṣṇa, the prince of cowherds, heard from the best of parrots that the *gopīs* were coming soon, He smiled slightly and carefully erected a toll-station with His chums on top of the hill at a huge place known as Śyāma-vedī. (15)

Notes: *gopa-rāja-nandanaḥ etena tasya dhīra-lali-ta-nāyakocita niścintatvaṁ dhvanitaṁ* "The word Gopa-rāja Nandana indicates Kṛṣṇa's carefree Dhīra-Lalita-aspect."

smerāṁ surakta paṭṭa bhūṣaṇa bhūṣitāṅgīṁ
mūrdhniṁ sphurat saghṛta hema ghaṭīṁ vahantīm
sārddhaṁ tathāvidha sakhī nivahena rādhām
āntīṁ marāla-gati cāru lalāpa paśyan

agre pūrṇa vidhuṁ tad antara
lasad bandhūka puṣpa dvàyaṁ
madhye nistala dāḍimī phala-yugaṁ
bhaṅgyā prakāśya kṣaṇam
man netrasya cakora bhṛṅga śukatām āsādayantyadbhutā
keyaṁ mām api padminī kṛtavatī raktaṁ marālaṁ drutam

smerāṁ - smiling; *su* - nice; *rakta* - red; *paṭṭa* - silken; *bhūṣaṇa* - ornaments; *bhūṣita* - decorated; *aṅgīṁ* - female body; *mūrdhniṁ* - on the head; *sphurat* - manifest *sa* - with; *ghṛta* - ghī; *hema* - golden; *ghaṭīṁ* - pots; *vahantīm* - carrying; *sārddhaṁ* - with; *tathāvidha* - similar; *sakhī nivahena* - with Her girlfriends; *rādhāṁ* - Rādhā; *yāntīṁ* - they go; *marāla* - swan; *gati* - slow gait; *cāru* -beautiful; *lalāpa* - prattling; *paśyan* - seeing. *agre* - above the *vigraha*; *pūrṇa* - full; *vidhuṁ* - moon; *tad* -that; *antara* - inside; *lasad* - beautiful; *bandhūka puṣpa dvayaṁ* - two Bandhūka-flowers; *madhye* - in the middle; *nistala* - round; *dāḍimī phala-yugam* - two pomegranates; *bhaṅgyā* - with a gesture; *prakāśya* - manifesting; *kṣaṇam* - moment; *mad* - my; *netrasya* - of the eye; *cakora* - Cakora bird; *bhṛṅga* - bee; *śukatām* - becoming a parrot; *āsādayanti* - causing to become; *adbhutā* - wonderful (fem.); *kā* - who (fem.) *iyaṁ* - this; *mām* - Me; *api* - even; *padminī* - Padminī-heroine, or lotus-vine; *kṛtavatī* - who makes; *raktaṁ* - red colour, or attachment; *marālaṁ* - lordly swan; *drutam* - swiftly.

Seeing Rādhikā slightly smiling, wearing a beautiful red silk *sārī*, decorated with different ornaments and carrying a golden pot with *ghī* on Her head, walking gracefully like a swan and surrounded by similar looking girlfriends, Kṛṣṇa said: "Which amazing Padminī (best of girls, or: lotus flower) has come before Me, turning My eyes into Cakora-birds eager to taste the nectar of Her moonlike face, bees eager to taste Her Bandhuli-flower-like lips and parrots eager to taste Her pomegranate-like breasts, and swiftly turning Me into a passionate swan that is eager to taste Her (like a lotus flower)?" (16-17)

Notes: *atra padminyāṁ vidhu-bandhūka-dāḍimānāṁ sarvathaivā'sad-bhāve'pi tad avasthāna-*

pradarśanāt tasyāḥ prathamam adbhutatvaṁ jñeyam. tathā marāla-netrasyāpi yugapac cakora bhṛṅga-śukatva-prāpaṇe'sambhavatvaṁ pradarśyā'pi dvitīyam adbhutatvaṁ dhvanitaṁ. tathā śukla-varṇa marālasya raktīkṛtatve'pi tasyā ananya sādhāraṇa śaktimattvena tṛtīyam adbhutatvaṁ jñāpitam. evaṁ cāsya śloka-ratnasya bahava eva dhvanayo niṣkāsitāḥ syur iti bodhyam —This verse is a jewel from which many meanings can be extracted: The first wonder is that this girl is compared to a Padminī, or lotus flower, and the items of Her body are compared to the moon, the Bandhūka-flowers and the pomegranates, all of which are inimical to the lotus flowers. The second wonder is that Kṛṣṇa, who compares Himself to a swan here, says that His eyes simultaneously become Cakora-birds, bees and parrots, and the third wonder is that the swan, who is naturally white, shows extraordinary power by becoming red (of passion).

tato nirīkṣya samyak tāṁ prema vihvala mānasaḥ
sāśaṅkaṁ paṅkajākṣo'yaṁ sotkaṇṭho'varṇayat punaḥ

phulla campaka vallikāvalir iyaṁ kiṁ no na sā jaṅgamā
kiṁ vidyul latikā-tatir na hi ghane sā khe kṣaṇa dyotinī
kiṁ jyotir laharī sarin nahi na sā mūrtiṁ vahet tad dhru-
vaṁ jñātaṁ jñātam asau sakhī-kula vṛtā rādhā sphuṭaṁ
prāñcati

tataḥ - then; *nirīkṣya* - seeing; *samyak* - properly; *tāṁ* - Her (with all above-mentioned special attributes); *prema* - love; *vihvala* - overwhelmed; *mānasaḥ* - mind; *sa* - with; *āśaṅkaṁ* - alarm; *paṅkajākṣaḥ* - lotus-eyed; *ayaṁ* - this; *sa* - with; *utkaṇṭhā* - eagerness; *avarṇayat* - described; *punaḥ* - again. *phulla* - about to blossom; *campaka vallikāvaliḥ* - vines of Campaka-flowers; *iyaṁ* - this; *kiṁ* - whether; *no* - certainly not; *na* - not; *sā* - She; *jaṅgamā* -

mobile; *kiṁ* - whether; *vidyut* - lightning; *latikā-tatiḥ* - a host of vines; *na* - no; *hi* - certainly; *ghane* - in the cloud; *sā* - She; *khe* - in the sky; *kṣaṇa* - momentarily; *dyotinī* - effulgent; *kiṁ* - whether; *jyotiḥ* - light; *laharī* - wave; *sarit* - river; *na* - not; *hi* - certainly; *na* - not; *sā* - She; *mūrtim* - form; *vahet* - carrying; *tad* - Her; *dhruvam* - certainly; *jñātaṁ jñātam* - I know, I know!; *asau* - this; *sakhī-kula* - girlfriends; *vṛtā* - surrounded; *rādhā* - Rādhā; *sphuṭaṁ* - clearly; *prāñcati* - splendidly approaches.

When lotus-eyed Hari carefully looked at Her with a mind overwhelmed with loving ecstasy, alarm and eagerness, He spoke again: "Is this a host of blooming Campaka-vines? No, because they don't move! Then is it a host of lightning-strikes? No, that also not, because they flicker in a cloud in the sky! Then is it a river-stream of effulgence? No, that is also not possible, because that has no form! Then I know for sure that it is Rādhā coming this way, surrounded by Her girlfriends!" (18-19)

Notes: *iyaṁ tu pratyaṅgaṁ lāvaṇyāmṛta-laharī-vistāriṇyapi vigraha-vatītyaho suvismayakaram* — "Although She extends a wave of nectarean elegance, She still appears in a distinct form - this is very astonishing!"

iyaṁ iha na ca rādhā sā sakhībhiḥ parītā
viditam idam idānīṁ vastu-tattvaṁ vicārya
mama savidham upaiti sphāra śṛṅgāra lakṣmīḥ
saha kalita suvarṣmāliṅganādi kriyābhiḥ

iyaṁ - this; *iha* - here; *na* - not; *ca* - and; *rādhā* - Rādhā; *sā* - She; *sakhībhiḥ*'- by Her girlfriends; *parītā* - surrounded; *viditam* - understood; *idam* - this; *idānīṁ* - now; *vastu-tattvaṁ* - actual truth; *vicārya* - considering; *mama* -

my; *savidham* - vicinity; *upa-eti* - approaching; *sphāra* - great; *śṛṅgāra lakṣmīḥ* - goddess of eros; *saha* - with; *kalita* - assumed; *su-varṣma* - beautiful body; *āliṅgana* - embrace; *ādi* - beginning with; *kriyābhiḥ* - with hallmarks.

"But actually, when I look carefully I see that it is not Śrī Rādhā surrounded by Her girlfriends, but the great goddess of eros Herself who has assumed a beautiful form and who approaches Me with Her hallmarks of kissing, embracing, biting the lips and so!" (20)

gaurī śrī vṛṣabhānu vaṁśa vilasat kīrti-dhvajā kīrtidā
garbhāntaḥ khani ratna-kānti laharī śrīdāma puṇyānujā
prāṇa preṣṭha sakhī nikāya kumudollāsollasac candrikā
mat prāṇoru śikhaṇḍi vāsa baḍabhī seyaṁ svayaṁ rādhikā

gaurī - golden beauty; *śrī vṛṣabhānu vaṁśa* - Śrī Vṛṣabhānu's dynasty; *vilasat* - shining; *kīrti* -fame; *dhvajā* - banner; *kīrtidā* - Kīrtidā-devī; *garbha* - womb; *antaḥ* - inner; *khani* - mine; *ratna* - gems; *kānti* - luster; *laharī* - wave; *śrīdāma* - Śrīdāma; *puṇya* - enchanting; *anujā* - younger sister; *prāṇa* - life-airs; *preṣṭha* - beloved; *sakhī* - girlfriend; *nikāya* - host; *kumuda* - lily; *ullāsa* - joy; *ullasat* - shining; *candrikā* - moonlight; *mat* - My; *prāṇa* - life-airs; *uru* - greatly; *śikhaṇḍi* - peacock; *vāsa* -abode; *baḍabhī* - a crooked stick to sit on; *sā* - She; *iyaṁ* - this; *svayaṁ* - Herself; *rādhikā* - Rādhikā

"It is Śrī Rādhikā Herself — the golden beauty, the beautiful banner of fame for king Vṛṣabhānu's dynasty, a wave of luster that came from mother Kīrtidā's jewelmine-like womb, Śrīdāma's charming younger sister, the most beautiful moonlight that delights Her lily-like girlfriends and the sittingplace for the peacock of My heart!" (21)

*tato govindam ālokya govardhana śiromaṇim
smitvā cāru calāpaṅgī tuṅgavidyedam abravīt*

*yaḥ kalkanair dadhi-ghaṭaṁ prakaṭam viluṇṭhya
nītvā pragāḍha tamasā milito'ti tṛṣṇaḥ
so'yaṁ girīndra śikharaṁ sphuṭam āruroha
rādhe tava priya sakho mahilaika cauraḥ*

tataḥ - then; *govindam* - Govinda; *ālokya* - seeing; *govardhana śiromaṇim* - Govardhana's crown-jewel; *smitvā* - having smiled; *cāru* - beautiful; *cala* - restless; *apaṅgī* - glances; *tuṅgavidyā* - Tuṅgavidyā; *idam* - this; *abravīt* - said. *yaḥ* - who; *kalkanaiḥ* - by quarrelling; *dadhi* - yoghurt; *ghaṭaṁ* - pot; *prakaṭam* - manifest; *viluṇṭhya* - stealing; *nītvā* - having taken; *pragāḍha* - dense; *tamasā* - with darkness; *militaḥ* - meeting; *ati* - very much; *tṛṣṇaḥ* - thirst; *sa* - he; *ayaṁ* - this; *girīndra* - Govardhana; *śikharaṁ* - peak; *sphuṭam* - clearly; *āruroha* - climbed; *rādhe* - O Rādhā; *tava* - Your; *priya* - dear; *sakhaḥ* - friend; *mahilā* - woman; *eka* - one; *cauraḥ* - thief.

When she saw Govinda standing on Govardhana Hill as its crown jewel, restless eyed Tuṅgavidyā smiled beautifully and said: "Rādhe! Look! Your dear friend, that woman-thief Giridhārī, has disappeared in the darkness after having openly stolen a yoghurt-pot during a quarrel and is now greedily climbing the summit of Govardhana Hill!" (22-23)

Notes: *tathāvidham tvat kāntam mahā-taskaram ati rasa-pipāsum jhaṭiti tvat savidham āgamiṣyantam paśyeti tasyāḥ uddīpanāya āśvāsanāya ca pūrva-vṛttām rati-līlām smārayati*— In this way Your lover is a great thief, and is very thirsty after *rasa*. Quickly go to Him. Just see, His past activities remind You of *rati līlā* and thus console You."

*mūrtiṁ nirjita nūtna nīrada balad garvonnatiṁ kaiśavīṁ
sphūrjad gopa-vadhū dhvanad dhṛti
camū dhvaṁse smarodyad gadām
vibhrājad giri-varya sundara
śiraḥ paṭṭe sphurantīṁ manāg
bhaṅgyāliṅgya dṛśā priyāli valitā rādhāpy adhīra'bravīt*

*kiṁ navyāmbuda eṣa bhavya-
vadanāḥ kiṁ nīla ratnāṅkuraḥ
kiṁ nīlotpala navya mūrtir api kiṁ kastūrikāvibhramaḥ
āsteṣv eṣa na ko'pi hanta
yad ayaṁ nas tāpayen nirbharaṁ tasmād gokula-candra
eva bhavitā śyāmo'dbhuta kṣmā-dhare*

    mūrtiṁ - form; *nirjita* - defeating; *nūtna* - new; *nīrada* - cloud; *balad* - increasing; *garva* - pride; *unnatiṁ* - supreme condition; *kaiśavīṁ* - of Keśava - *keśavasya praśasta cikuravataḥ*; *sphūrjad* - shining (of pride); *gopa-vadhū* - gopīs; *dhvanad* - resounding; *dhṛti* - patience; *camū* - armies; *dhvaṁse* - destroying; *smara* - Cupid; *udyad* - raised; *gadām* - club; *vibhrājad* - shining; *giri* - mountain; *varya* - greatest; *sundara* - beautiful; *śiraḥ* - crest; *paṭṭe* - on the slab; *sphurantīṁ* - shiningly manifest; *manāk* - slightly; *bhaṅgyā* - with movements; *āliṅgya* - embracing; *dṛśā* - with one eye; *priya* - dear; *ali* - girlfriends; *valitā* - surrounded; *rādhā* - Rādhā; *api* - even; *adhīra* - impatient; *abravīt* - said. *kiṁ* - what; *navya* - new; *ambuda* - cloud; *eṣa* - this; *bhavya* - most beautiful; *vadanāḥ* - faces; *kiṁ* - what; *nīla* - blue; *ratna* - gem; *aṅkuraḥ* - sprout; *kiṁ* - what; *nīla* - blue; *utpala* - lotus; *navya* - new; *mūrtiḥ* - shape; *api* - even; *kiṁ* - what; *kastūrikā* - musk; *vibhramaḥ* - a kind of erotic pastime; *āḥ!* - O!; *teṣu* - in them (the cloud, sapphire, blue lotus and musk); *eṣa* - this; *na* - not; *kaḥ* - who; *api* - even; *hanta* - alas!; *yat* - because; *ayaṁ* - this; *naḥ* - us; *tāpayet* - afflicting; *nirbharaṁ* - greatly; *tasmād* - therefore;

gokula-candra - the moon of Gokula; *eva* - certainly; *bhav-itā* - will be; *śyāmaḥ* - bluish *adbhuta* -amazing; *kṣmā-dhare* - on the mountain.

While Śrī Rādhikā, who was surrounded by Her girlfriends, embraced that shiningly manifest form of beautiful-haired Keśava, that defeats the pride of fresh rain clouds in luster, that is like the club of Cupid lifted to smash the army of the *gopīs'* patience and that stood on the beautiful peak of Govardhana Hill, with the movements of one eye, She became impatient and said: "O Fair-faced girlfriends! Is this a fresh raincloud, a fresh sprout of sapphire, a new shape of blue lotus or some erotic pastime (incitement) of a musk perfume? No, it is none of these things, because they do not afflict us so much (with lust)! It must be wonderful Śyāma, the moon of Gokula, there on the hill!" (24-25)

Notes: *śyāmala-varṇa-sāmye'pi sarva vastu vilakṣaṇa-tāpa-dāyakatvād adbhutatvam iti vyañjitam* — "Although He is similar to them through His complexion, He remains distinct from all aforementioned bluish objects, because He gives us affliction. This is what makes Him amazing!"

vijita bhagaṇa dīvyat pūrṇa śubhrāṁśu śobhaḥ
sakhi-nikara vṛta śrīr nāpi kṛṣṇendur eṣaḥ
ayi pika madhu bhṛṅga smera mākanda yuktaḥ
smara nṛpatir upetaḥ svena vaḥ sandhi hetoḥ

vijita - defeating; *bhagaṇa* - stars; *dīvyat* - shining; *pūrṇa* - full; *śubhrāṁśu* - moon; *śobhaḥ* -beauty; *sakhi-nikara* - friends; *vṛta* - surrounded; *śrīḥ* - beauty; *na* - not; *api* - even; *kṛṣṇa-induḥ* - Kṛṣṇa-moon; *eṣaḥ* - this; *ayi* - O!; *pika* - cuckoos; *madhu* - honey, or spring; *bhṛṅga* - bees;

smera - smile; *mākanda* - mango; *yuktaḥ* - endowed; *smara* - Cupid; *nṛpatiḥ* - king; *upetaḥ* - coming; *svena* - by his own; *vaḥ* - you; *sandhi hetoḥ* - to meet.

"O! It is also not Kṛṣṇa-candra, for He defeats the shining full moon surrounded by His star-like friends! It must be that the great king Cupid has come here personally to meet You with his companions - the cuckoos, the spring (or honey), the mangoes and the bumblebees!" (26)

so'yaṁ goṣṭha mahendra paṭṭamahiṣī vātsalya līlākṛtiḥ
so'yaṁ gopa mahendra puṇya-viṭapī
prauḍhāmṛtodyat phalam
so'yaṁ prāṇa vayasya jīvita-ghaṭā rakṣaika
dakṣauṣadhaṁ
so'yaṁ dhenuka-mardi jīvita
jhaṣa sphārāmbudhir mādhavaḥ

saḥ - he; *ayaṁ* - this; *goṣṭha* - meadows; *mahā* - great; *indra* - king; *paṭṭa* - crowned; *mahiṣī* - Queen; *vātsalya* - parental love; *līlā* - play; *ākṛtiḥ* - form; *saḥ* - he; *ayaṁ* - this; *gopa* - cowherd; *mahā* - great; *indra* - king; *puṇya* - pious merit; *viṭapī* - tree; *prauḍha* - mature; *amṛta* - nectar; *udyat* - full; *phalam* - fruit; *saḥ* - he; *ayaṁ* - this; *prāṇa* - life-airs; *vayasya* - friend; *jīvita-ghaṭā* - life; *rakṣā* - protecting; *eka* - only; *dakṣa* - expert; *auṣadhaṁ* - medicine; *saḥ* - he; *ayaṁ* - this; *dhenuka-mardi* - the killer of Dhenukāsura; *jīvita* - life; *jhaṣa* - fish; *sphāra* - extensive; *ambudhiḥ* - ocean; *mādhavaḥ* - Mādhava.

"This Mādhava is the very form of Queen Yaśodā's maternal love, the ripe nectar-oozing fruit from the tree of Nanda Mahārāja's pious merit, the only medicine that can save the lives of His heart's friends, and the ocean for the fish-like heart of Balarāma, the killer of Dhenukāsura!" (27)

nirūpyaivaṁ śaśvad giridharam uru prema nivahaiḥ
tadā sāsra sveda snapita śubha varṣma smara-vaśa
muhuḥ kampāghāta skhalad acala dīvyad ghṛta-ghaṭīṁ
dadhārārtyā śaktyā sakhi kara sarojena sudati

nirūpya - seeing; *evaṁ* - thus; *śaśvad* - constantly; *giridharam* - Giridhārī *uru* - great; *prema* - love; *nivahaiḥ* - abundance; *tadā* - then; *sā* - She; *asra* - tears; *sveda* - sweat-drops; *snapita* - moistening; *śubha* - auspicious; *varṣma* - body; *smara* - lust; *vaśa* - controlled; *muhuḥ* - repeatedly *kampa* - trembling; *āghāta* - struck; *skhalad* - falling; *acala* - motionless; *dīvyad* - shimmering; *ghṛta* - ghī; *ghaṭīṁ* - jug; *dadhāra* - carrying; *ārtyā* - with difficulty; *śaktyā* - with power; *sakhi* - O girlfriend; *kara* - hand; *sarojena* - by the lotus; *sudati* - O beautiful toothed one.

Seeing Giridhārī again and again in this way, Śrī Rādhikā became overwhelmed with lusty desires and sprinkled Her beautiful body with tears and sweatdrops of great love. O *sakhi*! She trembled again and again, making the otherwise motionless jug on Her head swing, so She stopped it from rocking with Her lotuslike hand. (28)

nepathyālīṁ lalita lalitāṁ dāni varyocitāṁ tāṁ
dhṛtvā santaṁ dhvanita muralī patra śṛṅgādi juṣṭam
ghaṭṭī-pālaiḥ kalita lakuṭair veṣṭitaṁ mitra-vṛndaiḥ
paśyantyas tāḥ smita valitayā helayā cāru celuḥ

nepathya - ornaments; *ālīṁ* - series; *lalita* - lovely; *lalitāṁ* - making it lovely; *dāni* - tax collector; *varya* - the best; *ucitāṁ* - suitable; *tāṁ* - it; *dhṛtvā* - wearing; *santam* -

standing; *dhvanita* -resounding; *muralī* - flute; *patra* - leaf; *śṛṅga* - bugle horn; *ādi* - beginning with; *juṣṭam* - served; *ghaṭṭī* - toll station; *pālaiḥ* - by guards; *kalita* - wearing; *lakuṭaiḥ* - with sticks; *veṣṭitam* - surrounded; *mitra-vṛndaiḥ* - by friends; *paśyantyaḥ* - seeing; *tāḥ* - they; *smita valitayā* - smiling; *helayā* - with a neglectful smile; *cāru* - beautiful; *celuḥ* - went.

Śrī Śyāmasundara dressed and ornamented Himself like a most charming tax-collector, complete with resounding flute and horn and was surrounded by His tax-collecting friends that were holding sticks. Seeing Him like this, the *gopīs* smiled slightly and walked along in a beautiful way, pretending to ignore Him, smiling with contempt. (29)

Notes: This *bhāva* of the *gopīs* is described as follows in Ujjvala Nīlamaṇi: *grīva recaka saṁyukto bhrū-netrādi vikāśakṛt bhāvādīṣat prakāśo yaḥ sa hāva iti kathyate. hāva eva bhaveddhelā vyaktaḥ śṛṅgāra sūcakaḥ* "When the neck is bent or the eyebrows and eyes expand, indicating desires for *rati,* it is called *hāva,* and when these desires are clearly indicated it is called *helā.*"

mattās tā madhurair bhāvair madhurā madhumaṅgalaḥ
dṛṣṭvā smitvā'tha sakrodham uvāca madhu-mardanam

garvena phullam adhunā madhunā'ti mattā
mattālibhiḥ samam amanda-balā'balā'pi
gacchaty asau sphuṭam adatta karā hi rādhā
bādhāḥ kathaṁ na hi vayasya balāt karoṣi

mattāḥ - inebriated; *tāḥ* - they; *madhuraiḥ* - sweet; *bhāvaiḥ* - with feelings; *madhurā* - a special beauty in form; *madhumaṅgalaḥ* - Madhumaṅgala; *dṛṣṭvā* - having seen; *smitvā* - having smiled; *atha* - then; *sa* - with; *krodham* - anger; *uvāca* - spoke; *madhu-mardanam* - to Kṛṣṇa; *garvena* - with pride; *phullam* - blooming; *adhunā* - now; *madhunā* - by the honey-wine of youth; *ati* - greatly; *mattā mattālibhiḥ* - with her intoxicated girlfriends; *samam* - with; *amanda* - great; *balā* - force; *abalā* -women; *api* - even; *gacchati* - they go; *asau* - this; *sphuṭam* - clearly; *adatta* - not given; *karā* - hands; *hi* - certainly; *rādhā* - Rādhā; *bādhāḥ* - checked; *katham* - how; *na* - not; *hi* - certainly; *vayasya* - friend; *balāt* - by force; *karoṣi* - you do.

Seeing them in these sweet moods, sweet Madhumaṅgala laughed and angrily told Madhumardana (Kṛṣṇa): "O Friend! Just see how quickly these girls are passing by, holding hands with Śrī Rādhā, not caring about us, being intoxicated by pride (of their youthful beauty)! Why don't You stop them by force?" (30-31)

Notes: *madhu 'puṣpa-rasaṁ' mardayatīti madhu-mardana śabdasya vyutpattyā śrī rādhikā mukha-padma-madhu-matta-rasika-bhramaratvena tasyopanyāsaḥ tena ca mardana śabda sāhacaryāt tad adhara pāne balātkāro'pi dhvanitaḥ* — Here Kṛṣṇa's name 'Madhumardana' means: "He who extracts the juice (honey) from the flowers." He is the *rasika* bumblebee that is madly intoxicated by the honey from Śrī Rādhikā's lotus-face, and who forcibly drinks the honey of Her lips.

hariṁ jetuṁ śaktāṁ madana nṛpateḥ śaktim atulāṁ
bhramad ghaṇṭī dhvānāṁ gati vilasitais tāṁ sa kalayan
udañcan mārodyad bhrama vikṛtim āguṇṭhya kapaṭān
mṛṣā roṣād eva sphuṭam idam avādīt sahacarān

satyaṁ bravīti madhumaṅgala eṣa dhūrtā
dānaṁ nipātya mama yānti madoru garvāḥ

paśyādya darpam adhunā mama mitra-varga
ghṛnāmi dānam acirād aham eka eva

harim - lion, or Himself; *jetum* - victory; *śaktām* - power; *madana* - Cupid; *nṛ-pateḥ* - King; *śaktim* - power; *atulām* - unrivalled; *bhramad* - moving; *ghaṇṭī* - bells; *dhvānām* - sounds; *gati* - motions; *vilasitaiḥ* - playful; *tām* - that lion; *sa* - He; *kalayan* - seeing; *udañcat* - increasing; *māra* - Cupid; *udyad* - arising; *bhrama* - delusion; *vikṛtim* - transformation; *āguṇṭhya* - covering; *kapaṭāt* - duplicious; *mṛṣā* - false; *roṣād* - out of anger; *eva* - certainly; *sphuṭam* - clearly; *idam* - this; *avādīt* - said; *sahacarān* - to His friends. *satyam* - truth; *bravīti* - speaks; *madhumaṅgala* - Madhumaṅgala; *eṣa* - this; *dhūrtā* - shameless; *dānam* - tax; *nipātya* - ruining; *mama* - my; *yānti* - they go; *mada* - inebriated *uru* - great; *garvāḥ* - pride; *paśya* - look! *adya* - now; *darpam* - pride; *adhunā* - now; *mama* - my; *mitra-varga* - party of friends; *ghṛnāmi* - taking; *dānam* - tax; *acirād* - swiftly; *aham* - I; *eka* - only; *eva* - certainly.

As Śrī Rādhikā playfully walked by, Her swinging sash of bells announced Her victory over Hari, proclaiming Her to be king Cupid's incomparible potency. When Śrī Hari saw that His defeat by Her was inevitable, He concealed the signs of His increasing desires and loudly told His friends in false anger: "This Madhumaṅgala speaks the truth! These shameless girls have become intoxicated by pride and they try to ruin My taxation by just passing by! O My friends! Now watch My pride also! I'm swiftly going to tax them all alone!" (32-33)

śṛṅgāni vādayata bho muralīs tathālīḥ
samrakṣata sphuṭam itas tata eva yāntīḥ

rādhām ahaṁ kuṭila yauvata varya nāthāṁ
ruddhāṁ karomi sahasā bhujayor yugena

śṛṅgāni - horns; *vādayata* - play; *bho* - O!; *muralīḥ* - flute; *tathā* - then; *alīḥ* - these girls; *saṁrakṣata* - stop; *sphuṭam* - clearly; *itaḥ tataḥ* - here and there; *eva* - certainly; *yāntīḥ* - they go; *rādhām* - Rādhā; *ahaṁ* - I; *kuṭila* - crooked; *yauvata* - young; *varya* - the best; *nāthām* - mistress Rādhā; *ruddhām* - stop; *karomi* - I do; *sahasā* - suddenly; *bhujayoḥ yugena* - with the arms.

"O! Sound the bugle horns and flutes and stop the *gopīs* that are fleeing here and there! I am going to catch Rādhā, the queen of youthful crookedness, in My arms!" (34)

ghaṭṭīpāla sahasra varya subala tvaṁ tāṁ viśākhāṁ
haṭhād ghaṭṭī kuṭṭima paṭṭa rakṣaka sakhe citrāṁ tvam
atrojjvala abhya śreṣṭha vasanta campakalatāṁ tvaṁ
tuṅgavidyāṁ tathā vartma prekṣaka
lakṣa dakṣa lalitāṁ tvaṁ kokilāveṣṭaya

ghaṭṭīpāla - toll collectors; *sahasra* - thousands; *varya* - best; *subala* - Subala; *tvaṁ* - you; *tāṁ* - her; *viśākhāṁ* - Viśākhā; *haṭhād* - suddenly; *ghaṭṭī-kuṭṭima-paṭṭa* - toll station; *rakṣaka* - guard; *sakhe* - O friend! *citrāṁ* - Citrā; *tvam* - you; *atra* - now; *ujjvala* - Ujjvala; *sabhya* - assembly; *śreṣṭha* - greatest; *vasanta* - Vasanta; *campakalatāṁ* - Campakalatā; *tvaṁ* - you; *tuṅgavidyāṁ* - Tuṅgavidyā; *tathā* - then; *vartma* - road; *prekṣaka* - guide; *lakṣa* - 100,000; *dakṣa* - expert; *lalitāṁ* - Lalitā; *tvaṁ* -you; *kokila* - Kokila; *āveṣṭaya* - grab.

"O Subala! O best of thousands of tax-collectors! Immediately stop this Viśākhā! O friend Ujjvala,

guardian of the toll station! You hold Citrā! O Vasanta, best of our assembly! Catch Campakalatā and Tuṅgavidyā! O Kokila, best of hundreds of thousands of expert road-guides! Catch Lalitā!" (35)

smerair etaiḥ sapadi parito veṣṭyamānābhir ābhir
vāg āṭopaiḥ priya sakha kuleṣv āśu saṁstambhiteṣu
raṅgair bhaṅgyā kuṭila vacasaṁ rādhayā saṁstuto'sau
kṛṣṇaḥ kopād iva sakhi tadā garvitaṁ tam avādīt

nityaṁ garvini vanya vartmani miṣāt saṅgopya gavyādika
vikrīṇāsi śaṭhe tvam atra patitā bhāgyena haste'dya me
tvāṁ baddhoru manoja rāja purato
neṣyāmy avaśyaṁ tathā
prītyā yacchati mahyam eva sa yathā tāruṇya ratnāni vaḥ

    smeraiḥ - by smiling; *etaiḥ* - by them; *sapadi* - at once; *paritaḥ* - all around; *veṣṭyamānābhiḥ* - surrounded; *ābhiḥ* - by them, the *gopīs*; *vāg* - words; *āṭopaiḥ* - with pride; *priya* - dear; *sakha* - friends; *kuleṣu* - in the group; *āśu* - swiftly; *saṁstambhiteṣu* - stopped; *raṅgaiḥ* - with fun; *bhaṅgyā* - with movements; *kuṭila* - crooked; *vacasāṁ* - by the words *rādhayā* - by Rādhā; *saṁstutaḥ* - fully praised; *asau* - this; *kṛṣṇaḥ* - Kṛṣṇa; *kopād* - out of anger; *iva* - as if; *sakhi* - girlfriends; *tadā* - then; *garvitaṁ* - pride; *tam* - him; *avādīt* - said. *nityaṁ* - always; *garvini* - proud girl; *vanya* - forest; *vartmani* - on the road; *miṣāt* - on the pretext; *saṅgopya* - hiding; *gavya* - milk products; *ādika* - beginning with; *vikrīṇāsi* - You sell; *śaṭhe* - O cheater; *tvam* - You; *atra* - here; *patitā* - fallen; *bhāgyena* - with fortune; *haste* - in the hand; *adya* - now; *me* - me; *tvāṁ* - you; *baddha* - bound; *uru* - greatly; *manoja* - Cupid; *rāja* - king; *purataḥ* - in the front; *neṣyāmi* - I will take; *avaśyaṁ* - certainly; *tathā* - then; *prītyā* - with love; *yacchati* - giving; *mahyam*

- to Me; *eva* - certainly; *sa* - he; *yathā* - as; *tāruṇya* - youth; *ratnāni* - jewels; *vaḥ* - your.

"O Sakhi!", Sumukhī continued, "the cowherd-boys that smiled and surrounded the *gopīs* were swiftly baffled by their proud words, and Kṛṣṇa, who was praised by Śrī Rādhā's crooked, playful words, pretended to be angry and told Her: "O Proud girl! You are always coming down this forest-path, hiding the *ghī* and so that You want to sell! O Cheater, fortunately You fell into My hands today, so that I can safely bind You up and bring You before king Cupid, who will lovingly give Me the jewels of Your youth!" (36-37)

ās tvad vidhān apy abalā-gaṇān
kiṁ neṣyāmi tasyoru nṛpasya pārśve
dāsyāmi śikṣām aham eva
sākṣāt tad advitīyo vraja pattane'smin

āḥ - cry of anger; *tvad* - you; *vidhān* - like; *api* - even; *abalā-gaṇān* - weak women; *kiṁ* - whether; *neṣyāmi* - I will take; *tasya* - his; *uru* - great; *nṛpasya* - of the king; *pārśve* - by the side; *dāsyāmi* - I will give; *śikṣām* - lesson; *aham* - I; *eva* - certainly; *sākṣāt* - directly; *tad* - this; *advitīyaḥ* - unrivalled; *vraja pattane* - in the settlement of Vraja; *asmin* - within.

"Aha! Should I bring weak girls like you before king Cupid? In this Vraja-maṇḍala I am non-different from Cupid, so I will teach You a lesson Myself!" (38)

badhnāmi tūrṇam anayā vana-mālayā tvāṁ
mathnāmi hanta daśana-cchadam atra dantaiḥ
sandārayāmi kucayor yugalaṁ nakhāstrair
dānaṁ na cej jhaṭiti yacchasi caurike tvam

badhnāmi - I will bind; *tūrṇam* - immediately; *anayā* - by her; *vana-mālayā* - by the forestflower garland; *tvām* - you; *mathnāmi* - I will agitate; *hanta* - O!; *daśana-cchadam* - covering the teeth, i.e. lips; *atra* - here; *dantaiḥ* - by the teeth; *sandārayāmi* - I will scratch; *kucayoḥ* - breasts; *yugalam* - couple; *nakha* - nails; *astraiḥ* - by the weapons; *dānam* - gift; *na* - not; *cet* - if; *jhaṭiti* - immediately; *yacchasi* - you give; *caurike* - O thief (fem.)!; *tvam* - you.

"O Thief! If You do not quickly give Me My tax I will bind You up with this forest-flower-garland, bite Your lips with My teeth and scratch Your breasts with My nail-weapons!" (39)

ittham prajalpa rabhasāt tarasā tadīya
raktāmbarāñcalam analpaka cañcale'smin
dhartum samicchati ruṣā paruṣākṣaram tam
cañcad dṛg añcala-kalā sukalā lalāpa

dūreṣu tiṣṭha na hi mām spṛśa dhṛṣṭa dhūrta
yāntī suyāga bhavanam vratinīm pavitrām
spṛṣṭām tavādya marutā'pi madīya gavyam
śyāmībhavan na bhavitā śubha yajña yogyam

ittham - thus; *prajalpa* - speaking; *rabhasāt* - eagerly; *tarasā* - quickly; *tadīya* -her; *rakta* - red; *ambara* - garment; *añcalam* - edge; *analpaka* - greatly; *cañcale* - naughty; *asmin* - in this; *dhartum* -to catch; *samicchati* - desired; *ruṣā* - angrily; *paruṣa* - harsh; *akṣaram* - syllables; *tam* - unto Him; *cañcad* - restless; *dṛg* - glances; *añcala-kalā* - corner; *sukalā* - beautiful, benevolent or artistic in the sense of creative; *lalāpa* - spoke; *dūreṣu* - in the distance; *tiṣṭha* - stay; *na* - not; *hi* - certainly; *mām* - Me; *spṛśa* - touch; *dhṛṣṭa dhūrta* - shameless cheater; *yāntī* - they are going; *suyāga* - a good sacrifice; *bhavanaṁ* - abode; *vratinīṁ* - dedicated girls; *pavitrām* - pure; *spṛṣṭāṁ* - touching; *tava* - Your; *adya* - now; *maruta* - the wind; *api* - even; *madīya* - My; *gavyaṁ* - dairy products; *śyāmībhavan* - contaminated; *na* - not; *bhavitā* - will be; *śubha* - auspicious; *yajña* - sacrifice; *yogyam* - suitable.

"When naughty Kṛṣṇa used such words and eagerly and quickly wanted to grab the edge of Her red *sārī*, artful Rādhā cast Her beautiful, restless glances at Him and angrily spoke the following stern words: "O Shameless cheater! Stay far away! Don't touch Me! Don't instruct a pure girls like Me, that is under a vow and that is going to a sacrificial arena! If our *ghī* is even touched by the breeze coming from Your body it is contaminated and no longer fit for this holy sacrifice!" (40-41)

kāmārṇavocchalita gharma jalābhiṣekaiḥ
śuddho'smi kiṁ na kila paśyasi dīrgha netre
tasmāt tvayā saha mahojjvala nāma satraṁ
kartuṁ lasāmi samayā śubha dharma patnyā

kāma - lust; *arṇava* - ocean; *ucchalita* - rising; *gharma jala* - sweat; *abhiṣekaiḥ* - through showers; *śuddhaḥ* - pure; *asmi* - I am; *kiṁ* - what; *na* - not; *kila* - certainly; *paśyasi* - you see; *dīrgha netre* - wide eyed girl; *tasmāt* - therefore; *tvayā saha* - with You; *mahā* - great; *ujjvala* - brilliant, or erotic; *nāma* - named; *satraṁ* - sacrifice; *kartuṁ* - doing; *lasāmi* - I am manifest; *samayā* - with an equal female; *śubha* - auspicious; *dharma patnyā* - pious wife.

Kṛṣṇa said: "O Dīrgha-netre (wide-eyed girl)! Haven't You seen that I was purified by taking a shower of sweatdrops that came from the ocean of desire?

Actually I desire to complete the great erotic sacrifice with You, taking You as My auspicious *dharma patnī* (wife who shares all pious merit)." (42)

Note: *tava netrasya dīrghatvāt darśanaucityam asti, tathāpi tvaṁ na paśyasītyaho āścaryam!* "You should be able to see it because You have such wide eyes, but still You don't see this — how amazing!"

etāṁ vayasya mṛdu hṛdya vacaḥ prabandha
raṅgaiḥ surañjitataraṁ nitarāṁ vidhāya
dānaṁ gṛhāṇa nijam āśviti kokiloktam
āśrutya sasmitam ananta vicitra līlaḥ

savyaṁ karam subhaga savya kaṭau nidhāyā-
savyena kṛṣṭa paṭa sṛṣṭa mukhārddha-guṇṭhāṁ
śīrṣṇi sphuran nava ghṛtojjvala hema kumbhāṁ
bhaṅgyā bhramat smita dṛśaṁ sa jagāda rādhām

ghaṭṭī kuṭṭima sṛṣṭapaṭṭa nikaṭe rādhe ghaṭīṁ sthāpaya
prodyat saurabha sadma padma
pavanaiḥ śrāntiṁ kṣaṇaṁ vāraya
dīvyan navya sugavya dāna vilasal lekhaṁ muhuḥ kāraya
krūrasyāli kulasya dānam acirād ārāt svayaṁ dāpaya

etāṁ - this girl; *vayasya* - O friend! *mṛdu* - soft; *hṛdya* - pleasant; *vacaḥ* - words; *prabandha* - use; *raṅgaiḥ* - with fun; *surañjitataraṁ* - greatly delighted; *nitarāṁ* - constantly; *vidhāya* - accomplishing; *dānaṁ* - tax; *gṛhāṇa* - accept; *nijam* - own; *āśu* - swiftly; *iti* - thus; *kokila* - Kokila; *uktam* - speaking; *āśrutya* - hearing; *sa* - with; *smitam* - slight smile; *ananta* - countless; *vicitra* - wonderful; *līlaḥ* - pastimes; *savyaṁ* - left; *karam* - hand; *subhaga* - beautiful; *savya* - left; *kaṭau* - on the hip; *nidhāya* - placing; *asavyena* - with the right; *kṛṣṭa* - pulled; *paṭa-sṛṣṭaḥ* - cloth; *mukha* -

face; *arddha* - half; *guṇṭhāṁ* - covering; *śīrṣṇi* - on the head; *sphurat* - clearly; *nava* - new; *ghṛta* - ghī; *ujjvala* - shining; *hema* - golden; *kumbhāṁ* - jugs; *bhaṅgyā* - with gestures; *bhramat* - moving; *smita* - smile; *dṛśaṁ* - eyes; *sa* - He; *jagāda* - told; *rādhām* - Rādhā. *ghaṭṭī kuṭṭima sṛṣṭa-paṭṭa* - toll station; *nikaṭe* - close to; *rādhe* - O Rādhe! *ghaṭīṁ* - pot; *sthāpaya* - place; *prodyat* - rising; *saurabha* - scent; *sadma* - abode; *padma* - lotus; *pavanaiḥ* - fragrant breeze; *śrāntiṁ* - fatigue; *kṣaṇaṁ* - momentarily; *vāraya* - stop; *dīvyan* - brilliant; *navya* - fresh; *sugavya* - good dairy products; *dāna* - tax; *vilasat* - proper; *lekhaṁ* - writing; *muhuḥ* - again; *kāraya* - cause to do; *krūrasya* - of the cruel; *āli kulasya* - of the *gopīs*; *dānam* - gift; *acirād* - swiftly; *ārāt* - close by; *svayaṁ* - personally; *dāpaya* - cause to do.

When He heard Kokila say: "O friend! Quickly collect Your tax and please Śrī Rādhā even more by using soft and gentle words!" Kṛṣṇa, who plays countless wonderful pastimes, smiled slightly, placed His left hand on His beautiful left hip and pulled the veil from Rādhikā's head with His right hand, leaving Her head half uncovered. Then He told smiling-eyed Rādhikā, who wandered about making many gestures while carrying a glistening golden pot with fresh *ghī* on Her head: "Hey Rādhe! Place that pot close to the toll-station! Let the soft breeze, that carries the fragrance of lotus flowers, remove Your fatigue for a moment! Make a proper tax-declaration of the fresh *ghī* You carry and quickly bring me the tax that Your cruel friends owe Me also!" (43-45)

Notes: *yad vā — hṛdi 'kṛtvā' mṛdu yathā syāt tathā avacaḥ prabandha-raṅgaiḥ (vāg vihīnāśleṣa kautukaiḥ) —* Kokila may also mean: "Please Rādhā more by gently and blissfully embracing Her without speaking a word."

āgaccha he lipi-pate madhumaṅgaleha
pañjiṁ paṭhan dṛḍha-matiḥ kuru satya-lekham
utkoca lobha bharato yadi nāśayes tvaṁ
ravyāṇi me kila tadā bhavitā'si daṇḍyaḥ.

āgaccha - come; *he* - O!; *lipi-pate* - scribe; *madhu-maṅgala* - Madhumaṅgala; *iha* - here; *pañjiṁ* - the royal rule; *paṭhan* - read out; *dṛḍha* - strict; *matiḥ* - attention; *kuru* - do; *satya* - truth; *lekham* - record; *utkoca* - bribe; *lobha* - greed; *bharataḥ* - filled with; *yadi* - if; *nāśayeḥ* - destroy; *tvaṁ* - you; *dravyāṇi* - articles; *me* - My; *kila* - certainly; *tadā* - then; *bhavitā* - will become; *asi* - you are; *daṇḍyaḥ* - to be punished.

"O scribe Madhumaṅgala! Come here and attentively read out the king's decree! Record everything truthfully - if You ruin My taxation out of greed for a bribe, you are also punishable, remember that!" (46)

āgaccha kaccham avadhehi vidhehi lekhaṁ
dānaṁ nu dehi na hi dehi kaliṁ hi rādhe
vīṭīṁ ca bhuṅkṣva sarasaṁ kuru vaktra-bimbaṁ
puṇyāham ācara puraḥ samayaḥ śubho'yam

āgaccha - come; *kaccham* - near; *avadhehi* - pay attention; *vidhehi* - perform; *lekhaṁ* - writing; *dānaṁ* - toll; *nu* - indeed; *dehi* - give; *na* - not; *hi* - certainly; *dehi* - give; *kaliṁ* - quarrel; *hi* - certainly; *rādhe* - O Rādhe!; *vīṭīṁ* - betelleaves; *ca* - and; *bhuṅkṣva* - enjoy; *sarasaṁ* - juicy; *kuru* - do; *vaktra-bimbaṁ* - mouth; *puṇya* - auspicious; *aham* - day; *ācara* - behave; *puraḥ* - before; *samayaḥ* - time; *śubhaḥ* - auspicious; *ayam* - this.

"Hey Rādhe! Come here! Pay attention! Write out Your declaration and pay Your tax! Don't argue!

Colour Your mouth by chewing *pān* and act piously, for this is an auspicious day!" (47)

> *yasya yan niyata dānam amuṣya*
> *vastunaḥ sudṛḍham ucyate mayā*
> *tat tat eva kila likhyatāṁ tvayā*
> *yatnato likhana-śūra vayasya*

yasya - whose; *yad* - which; *niyata* - ascertained; *dānam* - tax; *amuṣya* - our; *vastunaḥ* - articles; *sudṛḍham* - correctly; *ucyate* - spoken; *mayā* - by Me; *tat tat* - those; *eva kila* - certainly; *likhyatāṁ* - written; *tvayā* - by you; *yatnataḥ* - carefully; *likhana-śūra* - best of scribes; *vayasya* - friend

"O friend, best of scribes! I will tell you the right value of all the different items, write them down carefully!" (48)

> *gavyasya bhavya vadane prati pātram atra*
> *dānaṁ kila prati janaṁ vraja sundarīṇām*
> *vṛndāni pañca vilasan nava hīrakāṇāṁ*
> *yat saubhagādikam alabhyam anena labhyam*

gavyasya - of dairy products; *bhavya* - beautiful; *vadane* - face; *prati* - each; *pātram* - vessel; *atra* - here; *dānaṁ* - tax; *kila* - certainly; *prati* - each; *janaṁ* - person; *vraja sundarīṇām* - beautiful girls of Vraja; *vṛndāni* - billion; *pañca* - five; *vilasat* - sparkling; *nava* - new; *hīrakāṇāṁ* - of the diamonds; *yat* - what; *saubhagādikam* - beauty (*samṛddhi gauravādikam* - increase of honour and pride); *alabhyam* - precious; *anena* - by him; *labhyam* - attained.

"O Fair faced girl! You must pay five billion sparkling new diamonds for each pot of *ghi* that the *gopīs* carry, for although good fortune (honour and pride) is rarely attained I'm the only one who is fit to have it (and enjoy it)!" (49)

Notes: *līlā vistāriṇīṁ vande sakhīṁ śrī lalitāhvayām; yat kṛpayā pravṛtto'yaṁ mūko'pi raho varṇane* "I praise Śrī Lalitā-*sakhī*, who expands the transcendental pastimes of Rādhā-Kṛṣṇa, and by whose grace I have begun to describe these intimate pastimes, although I am an ignorant fool."

From verse 49 to verse 84 each of Śrī Rādhā's limbs is being described, on the pretext of collecting tax. Here and there explicit puns are also made about intimate pastimes - these can only be appreciated by *rasika bhaktas* and are very grave.

sīmanta kānti vilasan nava rāga valgu
sindūrayos tapana kānta maṇīndra lakṣam
veṇī varālaka kulojjvala kajjalānāṁ
gārutmatendra maṇi mañjula lakṣa yugmam

svarṇārdha candra-nibha bhāla talasya subhru
śubhrāṁśu-kānta-maṇi lakṣam atuccha śobham
kastūrika racita bhāla viśeṣakasya
gārutmatair ghaṭita candramaso'rbudāni

sīmanta - part of the hair; *kānti* - lustre; *vilasat* - shining; *nava* - new; *rāga* - red; *valgu* -charming; *sindūrayoḥ* - of the vermilion; *tapana kānta* - Sūrya-kānta sun-stones; *maṇi* - gem; *indra* -king; *lakṣam* - 100,000; *veṇī* - braid; *vara* - best; *alaka* - hair; *kula* - host; *ujjvala* - brilliant; *kajjalānāṁ* - of the eye-liner; *gārutmatendra maṇi* - emeralds; *mañjula* - lovely; *lakṣa* - 100,000; *yugmam* -pair.

svarṇa - gold; *ardha* - half; *candra-* moon; *nibha* - like; *bhāla* - forehead; *talasya* - of the place; *subhru* - nice eyebrows; *śubhrāṁśu kānta-maṇi* - moonstones; *lakṣam* - 100,000; *atuccha* - great; *śobham* - beauty; *kastūrika* - musk; *racita* - made of; *bhāla* - forehead; *viśeṣakasya* - leaf-pictures; *gārutmataiḥ* - with emeralds; *ghaṭita* - made; *candramaso* - moons; *arbudāni* - billions.

"For the beautiful red lustre of Your *sindūra* and Your part I want a hundred thousand sunstones and for Your braid, Your excellent curly locks and Your glistening eyeliner I want a hundred thousand sapphires and a hundred thousand emeralds (that are equally dark). For Your golden, halfmoon-like forehead I want a hundred thousand very beautiful moonstones and for the musk *tilaka* on that forehead I want billions of jewel-studded moons!" (50-51)

Notes: *atra pūrvārdhe sīmanta kānti sindūrayor anupamayor nyakkṛta lakṣa sūrya-kāntayor dānatvena rasika mukuṭa-maṇir utkaṭa lālasaḥ śyāmasundaraḥ kaṭākṣa-bhaṅgyā tat tad bhoga viśeṣam eva prārthayati.* By asking for a payment of one lakh of sun-stones, that defeat the matchless luster of Rādhā's hair-part and the red colour of the lustrous vermilion in it, with the gestures of His eyes, in the first half of verse 50, Rasika Mukuṭamaṇi Śyāmasundara, who is greatly agitated by desire, prays for the enjoyment of these items from Her. *parārdhe'pi marakatendra-nīla-mañjula maṇi vinindi veṇyalaka kajjalānāṁ viśeṣa bhoga eva bhaṅgyā prārthitaḥ.* In the latter half of the verse Kṛṣṇa uses puns to beg for the special enjoyment of Her braid and Her eye-liner, that mock the loveliness of emeralds and sapphires. *atredaṁ boddhavyaṁ - dāna-ślokeṣu prāyaśaḥ upameyopamāyā dṛṣṭatvāt tasyāś ca upameya bhūtasya vastu jātasya upamāna vijayi vyatireka mukhena* *varṇanaucityāt sarvatraivopameyasya māhātmyātiśayas tathā rasa camatkārāvahatvaṁ ca sūcyatetarām iti - yad uktam alaṅkāra kaustubhe- upamānasya nindāyām ayogyatve niṣedhataḥ; upameyasya praśaṁsā sopameyopamā'parā.* Here it must be noticed that in the subsequent Dāna-*ślokas* usually the standard of comparison defeats the object of comparison. This is meant to create the astonishment of *rasa,* and is confirmed in Alaṅkāra Kaustubha — "It is because the object of comparison is in this case unworthy in comparison to its standard, which is therefore praised." *atra pūrvārdhe atyujjvala lakṣa candrakānta-tiraskāri lalāṭārdha candrasya svasya lalāṭa-stha candana candrena saha sammilana rūpa bhoga-viśeṣa eva svābhilāṣaḥ.* In the first half of verse 51 Kṛṣṇa reveals His desire for the half-moon-like forehead of Śrīmatī, that defeats the splendor of lakhs of brightly radiant moonstones, to meet with the sandalwood pulp and camphor situated on His own forehead. *parārdhe śrīmatyāḥ kapoladeśa-stha mṛgamada-racita-patra-bhaṅgaiḥ saha nāgara varasyāsīma lālasā-bharasyendranīla-nibha kapola-stha candana bindubhir milanam eva svābhīpsitam iti bodhyam* In the latter half of verse 51 Nāgara-vara uses suggestion to reveal His unlimited desire for the leaf-pictures of musk on Śrīmatī's cheeks to meet with the spots of sandalwoodpulp on His cheeks, that shine with desire like emerald mirrors.

> *bhrū yugmakasya kuṭilasya śarāsanāni*
> *san nīla-ratna racitāny ayutāni pañca*
> *karṇa dvayasya rucirasya manojña navya*
> *vaidūrya maurva dṛḍha sad guṇa puñja puñjāḥ*

bhrū - eyebrows; *yugmakasya* - of the couple; *kuṭilasya* - of the crooked; *śarāsanāni* - of the bow; *sat* - good; *nīla ratna* - sapphire; *racitāni* - studded; *ayutāni* - 10,000; *pañca* - five; *karṇa* - ears; *dvayasya* - of the couple;

rucirasya - of the pretty; *manojña* - enchanting; *navya* - new; *vaidūrya* - lapis lazuli; *maurva* - of the Mūrva-vine; *dṛdha* - firm; *sat* - good; *guṇa* - attributes; *puñja puñjāḥ* - abundance.

"For Your crooked eyebrows I want fifty thousand sapphire-studded bows and for Your pretty ears I want the strong strings of the Mūrvā-vine, which is made of lapis lazuli!" (52)

Notes: The Mūrva-creepers are just fit for making bowstrings. It is said in 'Jagannātha Vallabha' - *śrutir na ca jagajjaye manasijasya maurvī-latā:* "These are not (Rādhā's) ears, they are the bow-strings of the universal conqueror Cupid, that are made of Mūrva-vines!" *vaidūrya-maṇi-vinindi karṇa-yugalasya mahā-vilāsa-kālīnāḥ śītkāra-bhūṣaṇa-śiñjita kala-bhāṣaṇādaya eva bhaṅgī-viśeṣeṇa prārthitā:* By mentioning Her ears, that defeat lapis lazuli-stones, Kṛṣṇa hints through suggestions that He wants to hear Her shrieks during the climax of love-making, the jingling of Her ornaments and Her soft, sweet words.

kāmaṁ kaṭākṣa viśikhasya suparṇa ratna
san nirmitā daśa lakṣāṇi śarāḥ sutīkṣṇāḥ
akṣṇor yugasya subhagasya masāra sāra
nīlotpalāni niyutāni yutāni gandhaiḥ

kāmaṁ - enough; *kaṭākṣa* - glances; *viśikhasya* - of the arrow; *suparṇa ratna* - emeralds; *sat* - good; *nirmitā* - made; *daśa lakṣāṇi* - a million; *śarāḥ* - arrows; *sutīkṣṇāḥ* - very sharp; *akṣṇoḥ* - of the eyes; *yugasya* - of the couple; *subhagasya* - of the beautiful; *masāra* - sapphires; *sāra* - best; *nīlotpalāni* - blue lotusflowers; *niyutāni yutāni* - thousands; *gandhaiḥ* - with scents.

"For each of the sharp glances You cast at Me I want a million sharp emerald arrows of Cupid, for Your beautiful eyes I want thousands of fragrant blue lotus-flowers made of the best sapphires." (53)

Notes: *atra pūrvārdhe dhikkṛta marakata nirmita sutīvra śarāṇāṁ dānatvena viśeṣa surata-bhoga sādhakāni aṅgāni bhaṅgyā'bhilakṣyante. yad uktam alaṅkāra kaustubhe - ehīti pṛṣṭaga-sakhīkṣaṇa-kaitavena, vyāvṛtya yo mayi tayā nihitaḥ kaṭākṣaḥ; pratyastravan mama kaṭākṣam avāpya śānto'pyantar vibheda sa nikṛtta śarārddhavan me.* "By moving His different limbs in the first half of the verse, Kṛṣṇa indicates that with these very sharp arrows, that mock the emeralds, She will give His limbs special erotic enjoyment." Thus it is said in 'Alaṅkāra Kaustubha': "Come!, The retreating cheaters of My *sakhī*'s glances told Me, while She cast her glance at Me. When she received the retaliation from My missile-like glances She became peaceful, but still she pierced My heart like half an arrow.." *parārdhe ca indranīlamaṇi-jaṭita nīlotpala mardī nayanayor dānatvena sva nayana milanādi bhoga jātaṁ nayana bhaṅgyaiva prārthitam* "In the second half of the verse Rādhā's eyes defeat the beauty of blue lotuses made of sapphires, and by giving them to Kṛṣṇa, She makes His eyes enjoy the bliss of meeting Hers. For this He prays on the pretext of mentioning Her eyes."

kārtasvarair ghaṭita kīra kiśora cañcu
puñjaḥ prakṛṣṭa tila-puṣpa sunāsikāyāḥ
sad gaṇḍayor madhura kāñcana darpaṇānāṁ
vṛndaṁ nava sphaṭikato'py ati cikkaṇānām

kārtasvaraiḥ - with gold; *ghaṭita* - fashioned; *kīra* - parrot; *kiśora* - adolescent; *cañcu* - beaks; *puñjaḥ* - a multitude; *prakṛṣṭa* - excellent; *tila-puṣpa* - sesame flower; *su* -

nice; *nāsikāyāḥ* - of the nose; *sad* - good; *gaṇḍayoḥ* - cheeks; *madhura* - sweet; *kāñcana* - gold; *darpaṇānāṁ* - of the mirror; *vṛndaṁ* - multitude; *nava* - new; *sphaṭikataḥ* - than crystal; *api* - even; *ati* - great; *cikkaṇānām* - glossy.

"For Your most beautiful nose, that resembles a sesame-flower, I want the golden beaks of many young parrots and for Your beautiful cheeks I want a billion golden mirrors that are smoother than new crystals!" (54)

Notes: *pūrvārdhe dhikkṛta svarṇa jaṭita śuka cañcū-rūpāyāḥ, tila-puṣpa-vijayinyāḥ kandarpādbhuta tūna-yuga-yuta nāsikāyāḥ suratottha parimalāsvādanādikaṁ nāsikā bhaṅgyā sūcitam.* By moving His nose and mentioning Rādhikā's nose, that mocks the golden beaks of parrots, the sesame flowers, and the two wonderful quivers of Cupid in the first half of the verse Kṛṣṇa hints that He wants His nose to enjoy the fragrance that arises from love-making. *parārdhe nyakkṛta nava sphaṭika-kāñcana-darpaṇayor gaṇḍayoḥ cumbanādikaṁ svābhipretaṁ svādharauṣṭha-bhaṅgyā jñāpitam* In the latter half of the verse Kṛṣṇa moves His lips to indicate that He wants to kiss Her cheeks, that mock new crystals and golden mirrors."

sarvopamā mahima-mardi mukhasya pūrṇa
śubhrāṁśu lakṣam atha phulla saroja lakṣam
uddāma dhāma maṇi darpaṇa lakṣam atra
sauvarṇam eva cibukasya ca ratna puñjaḥ

sarva - all; *upamā* - comparisons; *mahima* - glories; *mardi* - defeating; *mukhasya* - of the face; *pūrṇa* - full; *śubhrāṁśu* - moon; *lakṣam* - 100,000; *atha* - and; *phulla* - blooming; *saroja* - lotus; *lakṣam* - 100,000; *uddāma-dhāma* - splendid; *maṇi* - jewelled; *darpaṇa* - mirror; *lakṣam* -

100,000; *atra* - here; *sauvarṇam* - golden; *eva* - certainly; *cibukasya* - of the cheek; *ca* - and; *ratna* - jewels; *puñjaḥ* - abundance.

"For Your face, that shatters all comparisons, I want a hundred thousand full moons, a hundred thousand blooming lotus flowers and a hundred thousand glistening jewel-studded mirrors, and for Your chin I want heaps and heaps of jewels!" (55)

Notes: *asaṅkhyāta pūrṇa-candra-praphulla-kamala-maṇi-darpaṇādi-vijayinaḥ atulanīyasya mukhasya dānatvena cumbanādi mahotsava rūpaṁ paramānanda jātaṁ mukha bhaṅgyā samprārthitaṁ. yad uktam alaṅkāra kaustubhe - aṅkāṅki skhalanaṁ karākari manaḥ samvāda samvedanaṁ karṇākarṇi vṛthā kathāsu yugapac cumbāḥ śatam gaṇḍayor ityādi.* With His mouth Kṛṣṇa indicates to Rādhā that by giving Him Her matchless face, that defeats innumerable full moons, blossoming lotus flowers, jewelled mirrors and other items, She will give Him topmost ecstasy in the form of a great festival of kisses. Thus it is said in 'Alaṅkāra Kaustubha': "They fall from Each other's laps, touch Each other with the hands and talk to Each other about what is on Their minds. They speak nonsense into Each others' ears and kiss Each other on the cheeks a hundred times, simultaneously!" *tathā ratna-puñja tiraskāri cibukasya ca bhaṅgīkrameṇa tāruṇya-ratnāsvādo vā sparśa-sukha eva vā-bhipretaḥ* — By mentioning Her chin, that defeats heaps of jewels, He indicates that He wishes to relish the bliss of Her touch, or of the jewels of Her youth."

*bimbādharasya madhurasya surāga-padma
rāgaikapadmam iha padma-vara prabhāyāḥ
sampakka dāḍima phalojjvala bīja nindi
dantāvaleḥ śikhara laksam adṛṣṭa kakṣam*

bimba - a type of cherry; *adharasya* - of the cheek; *madhurasya* - of the sweet; *su* - nice; *rāga*-red; *padma-rāga* - lotus; *eka* - one; *padmam* - lotus; *iha* - here; *padma-vara* - the best of lotuses; *prabhāyāḥ* - of the luster; *sampakka* - fully ripened; *dāḍima* - pomegranate; *phala* - fruits; *ujjvala* - brilliant; *bīja* - seed; *nindi* - mocking; *dantāvaleḥ* - row of teeth; *śikhara* - a gem; *lakṣam* - 100,000; *adṛṣṭa-kakṣam* - the class of the unseen (incomparible).

"For Your sweet lips, that shine like Bimba-fruits and red lotusflowers, I want ten billion rubies and for Your teeth, that shine like pomegranate-seeds, I want a hundred thousand incomparible Māṇikya-jewels!" (56)

Notes: *pūrvārdhe lakṣa padma-rāga-vinindi bimbādharasyātulanīya sudhāsvādanam eva sva rasanā bhaṅgyā prārthitam.* In the first half of the verse Kṛṣṇa moves His tongue, indicating His desire to relish the nectar from Rādhikā's matchless Bimba-cherry-like lips, that mock lakhs of rubies. *parārdhe śikhara māṇikya vijayi dantāvaleḥ dānam tu vaiparītyena svādhara damśanas tathā svābhiyoga prakāśanāya śrī rādhayā kṛta svādhara-damśa-rūpāpūrvāsvāda viśeṣa eva vā bhaṅgyā'bhilakṣitaḥ* —"In the latter half Kṛṣṇa prays to Rādhā through hints that She will give Him Her teeth, that defeat the Śikhara-gems, but in the reverse pastimes He prays through gestures that She will give Him a wonderfully nectarean relish by biting His lips with Her teeth. To reveal this pun He bites His own lips."

so'yaṁ tvad vadanāravinda cibuke kastūrikā kalpitaḥ
samyak sundara bindur indu-vadane
niḥsaṅga bhṛṅgo mataḥ
sa smerāṁ mama dṛṅ milan
madhukarīm āliṅgatu premataḥ
satyaṁ dānam idaṁ priye nahi paraṁ kiñcin mayā yācate

saḥ - he; *ayaṁ* - this; *tvad* - Your; *vadanāravinda* - lotusface; *cibuke* - on the cheek; *kastūrikā* - musk; *kalpitaḥ* - decorated; *samyak* - properly; *sundara* - beautiful; *binduḥ* - drop; *indu-vadane* - moon-face; *niḥsaṅga* - solitary; *bhṛṅgaḥ* - bumblebee; *mataḥ* - like; *sa* - he; *smerāṁ* - smile; *mama* - my; *dṛk* - glance; *milat* - meeting; *madhukarīm* - honeybee; *āliṅgatu* - may embrace; *premataḥ* - out of love; *satyaṁ* - true; *dānam* - tax; *idam* - this; *priye* - O dear; *nahi* - not; *paraṁ* - greater; *kiñcit* - slightly; *mayā* - by Me; *yācate* - prayed.

"O Indu-vadane (moonfaced girl)! The very beautiful musk-drop on the chin of Your lotus-like face looks just like a lonely blackbee! Let that blackbee embrace My smiling bee-girl-like eyes with love. I don't pray for anything else!" (57)

Notes: *mṛga-mada-bindoḥ nirantara sva dṛg gocarī karaṇam eva mahā-surata-lāsyoddīpikam iti spaṣṭoktyā'bhiyācitam* "With clear words Kṛṣṇa prays here for great erotic dancing (love-making), being constantly incited in this by seeing this musk-drop."

gānāmṛtābdhi pariveṣaṇa dakṣa darvī
divyāti rakta rasanā ramaṇīyatāyāḥ
karpūra sāra parivāsita navya hṛdya
mādhvīka pūrṇa caṣakāvalir adya sadyaḥ

gāna - songs; *amṛta* - nectar; *abdhi* - ocean; *pariveṣaṇa* - serving; *dakṣa* - expert; *darvī* - spoon; *divya* - divine; *ati* - very much; *rakta* - red; *rasanā* - tongue; *ramaṇīyatāyāḥ* - of ever-fresh charming beauty, as it is said *kṣaṇe kṣaṇe yan navatām upaiti tad eva rūpam ramaṇīyatāyāḥ*; *karpūra* - camphor; *sāra* - essence; *parivāsita* - scented; *navya* - novel; *hṛdya* - pleasant; *mādhvīka* - honey-wine; *pūrṇa* - full; *caṣakāvaliḥ* - cups; *adya* - now; *sadyaḥ* - suddenly.

"For Your very red charming tongue, which is like a spoon that is expert in serving Me nectar from the ocean of songs, You must give Me many cups full of fresh, camphor-scented delightful honey wine." (58)

Notes: *saṅgīta sudhā pariveṣaka rasanāyāḥ dānaṁ tu vaiparītyena śrī rādhā-mukhāravindasya param āsvādya sīdhunā sva mukha-caṣakasya pūrṇīkaraṇādikam iti mukha-bhaṅgyā jñāpitam* "With a gesture of His mouth Kṛṣṇa makes it known that He wants the payment of Śrī Rādhikā's tongue, that serves Him the nectar of song, but in the reverse pastimes He wishes to satisfy the cup of His mouth with the most relishable nectar coming from Śrī Rādhā's lotus-like face."

> *phullībhavat smita lavasya sutāra mañju*
> *muktāphalair vihita kairava koṭir addhā*
> *pīyūṣa sāra paripūrita śātakumbha*
> *kumbhāyutaṁ masṛṇa mañjula jalpitasya*

phullībhavat - blossoming; *smita* - smile; *lavasya* - of the slightest; *sutāra* - brilliant; *mañju* - lovely; *muktāpha-laiḥ* - by pearls; *vihita* - placed; *kairava* - white lotus; *koṭiḥ* - ten million; *addhā* - directly; *pīyūṣa* - nectar; *sāra* - essence; *paripūrita* - filled; *śātakumbha* - golden; *kumbha* -

jugs; *ayutaṁ* - ten thousand; *masṛṇa* - soft; *mañjula* - love-ly; *jalpitasya* - of the words.

"The real price for Your blossoming gentle smile is ten million lovely sparkling white lotus flowers made of big charming pearls, and for Your tender and lovely words You must give Me ten thousand golden pitchers filled with the essence of nectar." (59)

Notes: *pūrvārdhe ananta vilāsa-sampādaka sāmagrībhiḥ saha vartamānāyāḥ śrī rādhāyāḥ sakāśaṁ svasya maugdhyāviṣkāreṇa vā sva-sanmukhaṁ samu-pasthāpitasya nikhila bhogya vastu-jātasya yathātyatham āsvādane nāgara śekharasyāpyanaipuṇya darśanād vā śrīmatyāḥ parama madhura smita lavasyodreka eva bhaṅgyā prārthitaḥ. parārdhe tad avasthāyāṁ mithaḥ kal-abhāṣitaṁ vā śrama vijaḍitam arddha sphuṭa vākya jātaṁ vā parama madhurātvenāsvādanīyam iti bhaṅgyā svābhilaṣitaṁ jñāpitam iti dik.* In the first half of the verse Nāgara Śekhara prays through gestures for Śrīmatī's sweet-est smile to arise even slightly when She sees His inability to properly relish all the countless enjoyable items that She placed before Him at present, thus revealing His bewilder-ment. In the latter half He uses gestures to reveal His desire to relish the sweetest nectar of an exchange of the sweetest, unclear words when They are exhausted of love-making.

> *śabdagrahoccalita sundara śātakumbha*
> *tāṭaṅkayor masṛṇa cumbaka ratnam ekam*
> *nāsāgra lagna nava kāñcana tantubaddha*
> *muktāphalasya ruci visphuritārkamālāḥ*

śabda-graha - the ears; *uccalita* - restless; *sundara* - beautiful; *śātakumbha* - gold; *tāṭaṅkayoḥ* - earrings; *masṛṇa* - fine; *cumbaka ratnam* - magnet; *ekam* - one; *nāsāgra* - tip of the nose; *lagna* - attached; *nava* - new; *kāñcana* - golden; *tantu* - network; *baddha* - bound; *muktāphalasya* - of a pearl; *ruci* - luster; *visphurita* - shining; *ārka-mālāḥ* - crystal gems.

"For Your very beautifully swinging golden earrings You must pay Me a very soft Cumbaka-gem (magnet, or a kiss) and for the pearl that hangs under Your nose on a jewel-studded golden string You must give Me a shining crystal necklace!" (60)

Notes: *pūrvārdha ayaskānta-maṇi-vijayinoḥ cañcalyamānayoḥ karṇa tāṭaṅkayor dānaṁ tu vilāsa viśeṣāvasthāyāṁ gaṇḍa deśe mṛdu cumbanādikaṁ svābhipretaṁ mukha bhaṅgyā jñāpitaṁ.* In the first half of the verse Kṛṣṇa indicates with a gesture from His mouth His desire to be softly kissed on the cheeks by Her in a special condition of love-making, on the pretext of taxing Her for Her beautifully dangling earrings, that defeat the magnets. *parārdha atyujjvala sphaṭika-vijayinaḥ nāsāgra bilan muktāphalasya dānaṁ tu vaiparītyena muktāphalasya sundara nartana darśanam eva bhaṅgyā'bhikāṅkṣitam* In the latter half of the verse Kṛṣṇa uses gestures to reveal His desire to see Rādhikā's nose-pearl beautifully dancing during reverse pastimes, on the pretext of levying ax on Her nose-pearl, that defeats the very brilliant crystal-stones and that dangles from a hole in the tip of Her nose..

> *surabhi vadana raṅge mugdha-gandhaṁ yadā te*
> *sphurita mṛdula cālaṁ cāru tāmbūlam utkam*
> *naṭati lalita raṅgais tasya dānaṁ tadānīm*
> *naṭanabhuvi madāsye'py āśu sannartayeti*

surabhi - fragrant; *vadana* - face; *raṅge* - on the stage; *mugdha* - enchanting; *gandhaṁ* - fragrance; *yadā* - when; *te* - your; *sphurita* - manifested; *mṛdula cālaṁ* - in a gentle way; *cāru* - beautiful; *tāmbūlam* - betelleaves; *utkam*

- eagerly; *naṭati* - dances; *lalita* - lovely; *raṅgaiḥ* - with playfulness; *tasya* - His; *dānaṁ* - taxation; *tadānīṁ* - now; *naṭana-bhuvi* - on the dancing stage; *mad* - My; *āsye* - in the mouth; *api* - even; *āśu* - swiftly; *sannartayeti* - causes to dance.

"When Your tasty fragrant *pān* softly and sweetly dances on the fragrant stage of Your mouth I request You to quickly make it dance on the stage of My mouth as well! That will be Your levy on this *pān*." (61)

Notes: *atra prāṇeśvaryānana candraga-sudhā-digdha saṁcarvita tāmbūlānāṁ muhur āsvādana viśeṣa eva prakaṭaṁ parimṛgyate* "Here Kṛṣṇa reveals His desire to repeatedly relish the special taste of betelleaves, laced with nectar-camphor, from the mouth of His Prāṇeśvarī Rādhā.

> *kambu śriyā kalita kaṇṭha-varasya hema*
> *śaṅkhāvalir valita valgu bhuja dvayasya*
> *svarṇollasan masṛṇa mañju mṛṇāla pālir*
> *vaidūrya paṅkaja-tatiḥ karayor dvayoś ca*

kambu - conchshell (with three lines on it); *śriyā* - with the beauty; *kalita* - endowed with; *kaṇṭha* - neck; *varasya* - of the best; *hema* - golden; *śaṅkhāvaliḥ* - of bangles; *valita* - round; *valgu* - charming; *bhuja* - arm; *dvayasya* - of the pair; *svarṇa* - golden; *ullasat* - beautiful; *masṛṇa* - fine; *mañju* - elegant; *mṛṇāla* - lotusstems; *pāliḥ* - abundance; *vaidūrya* - lapis lazuli; *paṅkaja-tatiḥ* - lotusflowers; *karayoḥ* - hands; *dvayoḥ* - of the couple; *ca* - and.

"For Your neck, that is as beautiful as a conchshell, You must pay Me with golden conchshells, for Your lovely round arms glistening smooth charming golden lotusstems and for Your hands with lotus flowers inset with lapis lazuli." (62)

Notes: *atra hema śaṅkhāvali vinindi kaṇṭhasya vilāsa viśeṣāvasthāyāṁ sva bhuja-dvandvena veṣṭanam eva bāhu bhaṅgyā dyotitaṁ, tathā suvartulasya bala-śālino vā bāhu-dvayasya vaiparītyena parirambhaṇādikaṁ sambhoga-jātaṁ samprārthitaṁ tathā karābhyāṁ puruṣāyita-bhāvena tayā sva-vakṣoja-manthanaṁ vā tasyāḥ kuca mardane anipuṇasya svasya hastopari taddhasta-yugalaṁ nidadhatyāḥ priyatamāyāḥ uparyadho-bhāvenaivāṅga-dvayasyā svāda viśeṣo vā bhaṅgyā samprārthitaḥ* : Here Kṛṣṇa makes a gesture with His arm that He wishes to embrace Her neck, that mocks the golden conchshells, with this arms during a special pastime (*rati vilāsa*). Then He prays that He may embrace Her with His round powerful arm during the reverse pastimes. Then He wants to place His hands on Her hands (to guide Her), seeing that She is inapt in massaging Her own breasts as She assumes the male role and They are situated upside-down. Through gestures He begs Her for this special relish.

hastāṅgulī samudayasya manoharasya
gandhonnataḥ kanaka bandhura gandha-phalyaḥ
pṛṣṭha-sthalī puraṭa sundara paṭṭikāyāḥ
kuñje prasūna śayane svapanādi keliḥ

hastāṅgulī - finger; *samudayasya* - of the host; *manoharasya* - of the charming; *gandha* - scent; *unnataḥ* - elevated; *kanaka* - golden; *bandhura* - beautiful; *gandha-phalyaḥ* - Campaka-buds; *pṛṣṭha-sthalī* - back; *puraṭa* - golden; *sundara* - beautiful; *paṭṭikāyāḥ* - of the plate; *kuñje* - in the grove; *prasūna* - flower; *śayane* - on the bed; *svapanādi* - by sleeping and other things; *keliḥ* - plays.

"For Your beautiful fingers You must pay Me with beautiful fragrant golden Campaka-buds, and for Your back, that is like a beautiful golden slab, You must

pay Me with pastimes on a bed of flowers in the *nikuñ-ja!*" (63)

Notes: *pūrvārdhe sugandha-kanaka-campaka-vinindi-hastāṅgulībhiḥ puruṣāyitena nakhāṅka dānādi sambhoga-nicayaḥ bhaṅgyā prārthitaḥ. parārdhe pṛṣṭhāpṛṣṭhi śayānayor mānavatyoḥ śvāsa-praśvāsādi prasaṅgaiḥ sparśa-sukha viśeṣa eva vā vilāsa viśeṣāvasara-smāra-spṛṣṭhastha nakhāṅka kajjalādi cihna yukta bhoga viśeṣo vā'tra svābhilāṣaḥ.* In the first half of the verse Kṛṣṇa makes gestures, begging for erotic enjoyment, in which the nails on Rādhā's fingers, that defeat golden fragrant Campaka-flowers, make scratching-marks on His body in a masculine way (during *viparīta vilāsa*). In the latter half of the verse They lie with Their backs towards Each other, in a state of amorous pique and Kṛṣṇa desires the blissful touch of Mānavatī's outgoing breath, or: the nailmarks on the back, that are reminiscent of special enjoyments, and the special enjoyments that involve marks of eyeliner, are here desired.

matta dvipendra mada gandhita kumbha yugma
garva prahāri kuca kumbha yugasya tasya
haimāni mañjumukhi dāḍima bilvatāla
sad dhāma nistala lalāma phalāni lakṣam

matta - maddened; *dvipa* - elephants; *indra* - king; *mada* - fluid that the elephant sweats out when he is lusty; *gandhita* - aromatic; *kumbha* - temples; *yugma* - pair; *garva* - pride; *prahāri* - removing; *kuca* - breasts; *kumbha* - jugs; *yugasya* - of the couple; *tasya* - his; *haimāni* - golden; *mañjumukhi* - fair faced girl; *dāḍima* - pomegranate; *bilva* - Bael; *tāla* - palms; *sad* - true; *dhāma* - abode; *nistala* - round; *lalāma* - best; *phalāni* - fruits; *lakṣam* - 100,000.

"O Mañjumukhi (fair faced girl)! For Your breasts, that destroy the pride of *mada*-scented temples of elephants, You must give Me hundreds of thousands of golden pomegranates, Bilva-fruits, palm-fruits and many other kinds of good fruits!" (*mada* is a fluid that the elephant sweats out when he is lusty). (64)

Notes: *etad bhogas tu bahudhā sampadyatetarām iti kati khalu lekhyā. matta karirāja mādaka dāna vāri gandhi kumbha-yugātiśāyinoḥ suvṛtta kucayor api mṛgamada kuṅkumādi yuktatvena mahā mādakatva vidhāyaka bhoga viśeṣa eva vā kauṭilya lalita yuktāti surasanīya kucākṣepo vā'tra spṛhaṇīyaḥ yad uktam ujjvale - citraṁ cira sparśa-sukhāya cucuke kurvantam akṣi pramiyaṁ calekṣaṇā svinnāṅgulīkaṁ pulakāñcita śriyā savyena cikṣepa kucena keśavam— evam viśākhānandā stotre 102 śloke'pi draṣṭavyam— mañju kuñje mukundasya kucau citrayataḥ karam; kṣapayanti kucākṣepaiḥ susakhya madhunonmadā* "Such enjoyment comes in many kinds - how can all of them be described? The fragrance of musk and *kuṅkuma* on Your big, round breasts are more intoxicating than the ichor trickling from intoxicated lusty elephants. It is also desired to be hit by these delicious breasts, that are so lovely, yet crooked. It is said in Ujjvala Nīlamaṇi: Śrī Rūpa Mañjarī told Śrī Rati Mañjarī: "Sakhi! When Śrī Kṛṣṇa blissfully draws pictures on Śrī Rādhā's breasts His fingers start to sweat. When Śrī Rādhā sees that Kṛṣṇa is delaying Her eyes become restless and She thrusts Keśava far away by knocking Him with Her left breast, that is studded with goosepimples." So it can also be see in verse 102 of Śrīla Raghunātha Dāsa Gosvāmī's 'Viśākhānandada Stotram' —"In a lovely grove She becomes intoxicated with the honey of intimate friendship and strikes Kṛṣṇa's lotuslike hands with Her breasts while He is trying to draw pictures on them."

madhyaṁ keśari varya madhyam
iva yaj jyāyo-rasasyāspadaṁ
vādyat kiṅkiṇi rakta-vastra vilasad baddhaṁ valī ḍorakaiḥ
tasyorūtkaṭa dānam apy uru nṛpād yatnair mayā gopyate
yady ādau tava nīvi bandhana maṇiṁ
gūḍhaṁ kare me'rpayeḥ

madhyaṁ - waist; *keśari* - of lionesses; *varya* - the best; *madhyam* - the waist; *iva* - as if; *yat* - which; *jyāyaḥ rasasya* - of the erotic mellow; *āspadam* - the abode; *vādyat* - tinkling; *kiṅkiṇi* - waistbells; *rakta* - red; *vastra* - garments; *vilasat* - shining; *baddhaṁ* - bound; *valī* - of the three lines; *ḍorakaiḥ* - by the ropes; *tasya* - his; *uru* - great; *utkaṭa* - unlimited; *dānam* - gift; *api* - even; *uru* - great; *nṛpād* - than the king; *yatnaiḥ* - by endeavours; *mayā* - by Me; *gopyate* - may be concealed; *yadi* - if; *ādau* - in the beginning; *tava* - Your; *nīvi* - undergarments; *bandhana* - binding; *maṇiṁ* - gem; *gūḍhaṁ* - concealed; *kare* - in the hand; *me* - of Me; *arpayeḥ* - You place.

"Although Your waist is as thin as that of a lioness, You will have to pay Me a lot for it, for it is the abode of erotic mellows, beautified by jingling waistbells, a red dress and a sash in the form of the lines on Your belly. If You hide the jewel that shuts the string of Your girdle in My hand I will be able to hide it from king Cupid with care!" (65)

iyaṁ nīvi rādhe nija niviḍa bandhaṁ davayituṁ
bhavad bhītyā bhaṅgyā mayi vitanute yācana vidhim
tathā taṁ tūrṇaṁ tvaṁ davaya madanendūdayakṛte
yathā'sau tuṣṭyā te karam urukaṭau no racayati

iyaṁ - this; *nīvi* - undergarment; *rādhe* - O Rādhe!; *nija* - own; *niviḍa* - tight; *bandhaṁ* - bondage; *davayituṁ* - to remove; *bhavad* - Your; *bhītyā* - out of fear; *bhaṅgyā* -

slackening on the pretext of wishing to see Me; *mayi* - in Me; *vitanute* - extend; *yācana vidhim* - prayer; *tathā* - then; *taṁ* - this; *tūrṇaṁ* - swiftly; *tvam* - You; *davaya* - remove; *madana* - Cupid; *indu* - moon; *udaya-kṛte* - accomplishing the rising; *yathā* - so that; *asau* - this *mat savidhaṁ sphūrtiṁ prāptaḥ madana candraḥ iti aṅgulī-helanena nirdiśyate*; *tuṣṭyā* - with satisfaction; *te* - Your; *karam* - ray; *uru* - big; *kaṭau* - on the hip; *no* - not; *racayati* - arises.

"O Rādhe! This girdle of Yours prays to Me with different gestures to be loosened, being afraid of You, so quickly open it, so that the moonlike Cupid will rise and will not charge anymore tax from Your waist, being satisfied!" (66)

Notes: *yad vā - tava karaṁ viparīta vilāsena naḥ (mameti vaktavye bahu-vacanam ātmanaḥ ānandātiśayena guru manyatvāt) uru-kaṭau (viśāla kaṭi-deśe) racayati (yojayati) iti sarvatraiva svābhilāṣaḥ sphuṭaṁ varīvarti. asāv iti madana candraṁ kāmukāḥ kāminī-mayam iti nyāyena diśi vidiśi sphurantam aṅgulyā nirdiśyate.* "Or this may mean: In reverse pastimes You place Your hand on our (it is actually 'mine' but out of great ecstasy He thinks in plural terms) big hip." Thus He clearly reveals His own desire everywhere. 'Madana Candra' (the moon of Cupid) refers to lusty men who see the whole world filled with beautiful women. (Kṛṣṇa thinks that Rādhā is as lusty as He is) This He indicates with by pointing with His finger all over the place."

nābhi sphurad hrada tad utthita romapāli
vyālīḥ śiraḥ sphurita ratna sunāyakānām
vaidūrya mañjula masāra varābja-rāga
ratnāni tāni niyutāni nava kramena

nābhi - navel; *sphurad* - manifest; *hrada* - lake; *tad* -that; *utthita* - arisen; *romapāli* - torso-hairs; *vyālīḥ* - female snakes; *śiraḥ* - the head; *sphurita* - manifest; *ratna* - jewelled; *su* - beautiful; *nāyakānām* - of Nāyaka-gems; *vaidūrya* - lapis lazuli; *mañjula* - lovely; *masāra* - sapphires; *vara* - the best; *abja-rāga* - jewels; *ratnāni* - jewels; *tāni* - they; *niyutāni* - million; *nava* - nine; *kramena* - gradually.

"For Your beautiful lake-like navel and the she-snake-like hairs on it that are crowned with beautiful jewel-studded Nāyaka-gems, You must pay Me ninety thousand lapis lazulis, lovely sapphires and rubies!" (67)

Notes: *vaidūryāśma-sāra padma-rāga vinindi nābhi sarovara tad uttha roma rāji sundara nāyaka-maṇīnām ca dāna rūpena tat tat sthāna sparśa-darśanādikaṁ svābhilaṣitam bhaṅgyā sūcitam* Through gestures Kṛṣṇa indicates that the actual tax of Nāyaka-gems that She must pay is that She must allow Him to touch and see Her lake-like navel, that mocks the beauty of lapis lazuli and rubies, and the beautiful torso-hairs that arise from it.

san nīla paṭṭa paṭarañjaka mañju kāñci
sañcāra cāru caṭulocca nitambakasya
samprollasat puraṭa pīṭha navārbudāni
dānīndrakasya mama yogya varāsanāni

sat - excellent; *nīla* - blue; *paṭṭa-paṭa* - coloured garment; *rañjaka* - beautiful; *mañju* - lovely; *kāñci* - waist-bells; *sañcāra* - movements; *cāru* - charming; *caṭula* - beautiful; *ucca* - raised; *nitambakasya* - of the buttocks; *samprollasat* - shining; *puraṭa* - golden; *pīṭha* - thrones; *nava* - nine; *arbudāni* - a hundred million; *dānī* - toll collector;

indrakasya - of the king; *mama* - My; *yogya* - suitable; *vara* - best; *āsanāni* - thrones.

"For Your gracefully glistening, raised buttocks, that are beautified by Your nice blue silken *sārī* and for Your lovely sash of bells You must give Me nine hundred million golden thrones fit for Me, the king of tax-collectors, to sit on!" (68)

Notes: *atrāti sundara nitambasya dānatvena nṛtyāvasare vā vilāsa viśeṣe vā rati-līlā vinoda eva bhaṅgyā prārthitaḥ* —By asking Her for Her very beautiful buttocks Kṛṣṇa hints that He wants to enjoy them during dancing or love-making.

> *uru-dvayasya kanakaiḥ kṛta cāru rambha*
> *stambhāvalir dalita sat karabha prabhasya*
> *mañjīra mañjula raṇac caraṇāravinda*
> *dvandvasya rakta-maṇi nirmita pallavāli*

uru - thighs; *dvayasya* - of the pair; *kanakaiḥ* - by the golden; *kṛta* - fashioned; *cāru* - beautiful; *rambha* - banana; *stambhāvaliḥ* - trunks; *dalita* - defeating; *sat* - true; *karabha* - elephant's trunks; *prabhasya* - beauty of tapering roundness; *mañjīra* - anklebells; *mañjula* - lovely; *raṇat* - jingling; *caraṇāravinda* - lotusfeet; *dvandvasya* - of the pair; *rakta-maṇi* - rubies; *nirmita* - made of; *pallavāli* - leaves.

For Your hips, that defeat the beauty of elegant elephants' trunks, You must give Me charming golden trunks of banana-trees, and for Your lotusfeet, that have sweetly jingling anklebells on them, You must give Me sprouts made of rubies!" (69)

Notes: *pūrvārdhe suvartulayos tathā krama-krasima-yutayoḥ kari-kara vijayinoḥ uru-yugasya bhoga viśeṣa evābhilakṣitaḥ. parārdhe padma-rāga-yukta pallava vinindi caraṇa padmayoḥ dānaṁ viparīta vilāse svābhāvike vā'tidhīreṇa śabdāyamānasya mañjīrasya sumadhura dhvanibhiḥ paripuṣṭa surata vitānam eva.* In the first half of the verse Kṛṣṇa aims at the special enjoyment of Rādhikā's thighs, that defeat the beauty of the round and tapering trunks of the elephants. In the latter half Śrī Rādhikā increases and expands the enjoyment of erotic pastimes by giving Her lotusfeet, that defeat the beauty of ruby-sprouts, in the reverse pastimes, and by making Her anklebells gently and sweetly jingle,_

smara rasamaya rājat kṣīṇa tundasya tasya
ruciratara taraṅga prāya tiryag valīnām
ayi tad anubhavākhyaṁ ratna-yugmaṁ nakhānām
udayad aruṇa candra jyotiṣāṁ ratna candrāḥ

smara - Cupid; *rasamaya* - full of taste; *rājat* - shining; *kṣīṇa* - slender; *tundasya* - of the belly; *tasya* - his; *ruciratara* - more tasty; *taraṅga* - waves; *prāya* - usually; *tiryak* - crooked; *valīnām* - of the three lines; *ayi* - O!; *tat* - that; *anubhava* - anubhava; *ākhyaṁ* - named; *ratna* - gems; *yugmaṁ* -pair; *nakhānām* - of the nails; *udayad* - arising; *aruṇa* - red; *candra* - moon; *jyotiṣām* - light; *ratna* - gems; *candrāḥ* - moons.

"For Your beautiful slender waist, that is full of erotic flavours and that has three crooked lines on it that look like waves of beauty, You must give Me the two new Anubhava-jewels, and for Your toenails that shine like rising red moons, You must give Me shining jewel-studded moons!" (70)

Notes: *pūrvārdhe kṣīṇodara valīnāṁ ca vilāsa-viśeṣe darśana sparśanādikam anubhava-jātaṁ kāṅkṣitam. parārdhe vaiparītyena prāṇeśvarī-pāda-pallava-śekhareṣu līlā svayamvara-rasa-lābha evāti vāñchitaḥ* [9] In the first half of the verse Kṛṣṇa desires the experience of seeing and touching the three lines on Rādhikā's slender tummy during a special (erotic) pastime. In the latter half of the verse He desires the meeting with the tips of His Prāṇeśvarī's toes during reverse pastimes when She Herself has chosen Him (as a husband, and sits on Him).

phulla kāñcana samudgaka garva
dhvaṁsinos tava vareṇya jānunoḥ
kāñcana prakaṭitāṁ kaṭa-koṭiṁ
kāñcana prakaṭa dānam ānaya

phulla - shining; *kāñcana* - golden; *samudgaka* - baskets; *garva* - pride; *dhvaṁsinoḥ* - destroyers; *tava* - Your; *vareṇya* - excellent; *jānunoḥ* - the knees; *kāñcana* - golden; *prakaṭitāṁ* - made of; *kaṭa* - baskets; *koṭiṁ* - ten million; *kāñcana* - golden; *prakaṭa* - manifest; *dānam* - tax; *ānaya* - bring.

"For Your excellent knees, that destroy the pride of the luster of shining golden baskets, You must personally pay Me ten million golden baskets tax! (71)

Notes: *galita suvarṇa sampuṭa vijayi jānu yugasyātula madana rasa mādhurī pariposita līlā vilāsādikam atrābhilakṣyam* Here Kṛṣṇa means to say that He wants Rādhikā's knees, that conquer the sweetness of baskets made of molten gold, to increase the sweetness of sweet erotic pastimes.

hārādy alaṅkṛti cayasya manojña rāśmes
tvad sparśa-ratnam atulaṁ mṛdu kaṇṭha-lagnam

*tvat kiṅkiṇī balaya nūpura nikkvaṇānāṁ
kāmaṁ mahonnata maṇi-dvayam eva hṛdyam*

hāra - necklace; *ādi* - etc.; *alaṅkṛti* - ornaments; *cayasya* - of the multitude; *manojña* - charming; *rāśmeḥ* - of the ray; *tvad* - Your; *sparśa-ratnam* - touch-stone; *atulaṁ* - matchless; *mṛdu* -soft; *kaṇṭha* - neck; *lagnam* - touching; *tvat* - Your; *kiṅkiṇī* - waistbells; *balaya* - bracelets; *nūpura* - anklebells; *nikkvaṇānāṁ* - of the jingling; *kāmaṁ* - enough; *mahā* - great; *unnata* - elevated; *maṇi-* gems; *dvayam* - pair; *eva* - certainly; *hṛdyam* - pleasant.

For Your beautifully shining ornaments like Your necklaces You must give Me the matchless touch stone around Your delicate neck, and for the jingling of Your bangles, sash of bells and anklebells You must give Me the two highly raised jewels on Your chest (Your breasts)!" (72)

Notes: *yathā sparśamaṇi sparśena kṛṣṇāyasam api svarṇa varṇaṁ dadhāti, tathā śrī rādhā kaṇṭha-lagnaḥ sannapi svasya kṛṣṇa-varṇam vihāya nibhṛta nikuñja mandire vilāsa viśeṣe gaurī-bhavanaṁ samprārthitam* "Just as a black stone gives up its black color and turns into gold when touched by a touch-stone, similarly Kṛṣṇa gives up His black colour when He hangs around Rādhā's neck during the erotic pastimes in the solitary bower-house and becomes golden. This is what He prays for." *vyākhyāntaram saṅgatecchata - tad yathā — hṛdyaṁ (tasyāḥ hṛdisthaṁ) mahonnata 'vakṣoja' maṇi-yugalam eva muhur muhuḥ āsvāditum sākūtaṁ parimṛgyate* Another proper explanation is that He eagerly seeks to relish Her two raised, jewel-like breasts again and again.

*san nīla rakta vasana-dvaya kañcukānāṁ
prodyat prabāla nava mañju masāra mālāḥ*

tvac chārikā mṛga-vadhū mahatī mayūrī
līlābja nartana-tater vara ratnakoṭyaḥ

sat - good; *nīla* - blue; *rakta* - red; *vasana* - garments; *dvaya* - pair; *kañcukānāṁ* - of the blouses; *prodyat* - manifest; *prabāla* - coral; *nava* - new; *mañju* - lovely; *masāra* - sapphires; *mālāḥ* -garlands; *tvat* - Your; *śārikā* - female parrots; *mṛga-vadhū* - does; *mahatī* - a Vīṇā; *mayūrī* - peahen; *līlā* - play; *abja* - lotus; *nartana-tateḥ* - of dancing and other arts; *vara* - best; *ratna* - gems; *koṭyaḥ* - of the millions.

"For Your red petticoat, Your blue *sārī* and Your blouse and so on, I want a string of beautiful new sapphires inset with coral, and for Your she-parrot, fawn, Mahatī Vīṇā, peahen, playlotus and dancing I want millions of jewels!" (73)

Notes: *pūrvārdhe indranīla garva dhvaṁsi nīla vasanasya prabāla dyuti-hāri rakta vastrasya tathā kañcukasya ca dānaṁ vilāsa-viśeṣāvasthāyām etat trayāṇāṁ sva kare samarpaṇam eva bhaṅgyā prārthitam.* In the first half of the verse Kṛṣṇa prays through hints that Śrī Rādhā may place Her blue garment, that destroys the pride of sapphires, Her red garment, that steals the lustre of coral, and Her blouse in His hand during erotic pastimes. *parārdhe kasyacit svābhīṣṭa maṅgala 'śrī-aṅga' viśeṣasya darśana sparśanādi rūpaṁ sambhoga jātaṁ bhaṅgyā prārthitam iti jñeyam* In the latter half He prays through gestures that She may give Him the special enjoyment of seeing and touching Her auspicious Śrī Aṅga (beautiful body).

kāntyā yasya kṣiti vana giri grāma lokāḥ samastāḥ
sākṣāj jātāḥ subhaga vadane hanta jambūnadābhāḥ

*tasya bhrāmyad dyuti-bhara valad gandhaphalyāvalīnāṁ
jaitrasyoccaiḥ kanaka girayo gaura varṇasya koṭyaḥ*

kāntyā - of the lustre; *yasya* - whose; *kṣiti* - earth; *vana* - forest; *giri* - mountain; *grāma* - village; *lokāḥ* - people, or planets; *samastāḥ* - all; *sākṣāt* - directly; *jātāḥ* - manifest; *subhaga* - beautiful; *vadane* - face; *hanta* - alas!; *jambūnada* - golden; *ābhāḥ* - splendor; *tasya* - of this golden splendor; *bhrāmyad* - spreading here and there; *dyuti* - lustre; *bhara* - intensity; *valad* - increase; *gandhaphalyāvalīnāṁ* - of the Campaka-buds; *jaitrasya* - of the victory; *uccaiḥ* - greatly; *kanaka* -golden; *girayaḥ* - mountains; *gaura* - golden; *varṇasya* - of the complexion; *koṭyaḥ* - of millions.

"O Subhaga vadane (fair faced girl)! For Your golden lustre, that turns the whole earth, the forest, the mountains, the villages and the people golden, defeating the golden lustre of Campaka-buds that radiates everywhere, I want millions of golden mountains!" (74)

Notes: *atra kanaka-girayaḥ ityanena śrī rādhā-vakṣoja-yugalasyābhīkṣnyena āsvādana dānam eva sūcitam* "Here the words 'golden mountains' indicate Kṛṣṇa wishes the payment of the repeated relish of Śrī Rādhā's breasts.

*gaurāṅgāṇāṁ kamala ghusṛṇa prāya saurabhya sindhor
vātenāpi vraja-vanam idaṁ vāsitaṁ tanvatas te
etasyānyat kim api na mayā dṛśyate dāna yogyaṁ
yātāyātaṁ kuru sakhi sadā dānam etan madīyam*

gaura - golden; *aṅgāṇāṁ* - of the limbs; *kamala* - lotus; *ghusṛṇa* - of vermilion; *prāya* - usually; *saurabhya* - of fragrance; *sindhoḥ* - of the ocean; *vātena* - by the breeze;

api - even; *vraja-vanam* - the Vraja-forest; *idaṁ* - this; *vāsitaṁ* - scented; *tanvataḥ* - doing; *te* - Your; *etasya* - of this; *anyat* - another; *kim api* - indescribable; *na* - not; *mayā* - by Me; *dṛśyate* - seen; *dāna* - gift; *yogyaṁ* -suitable; *yātāyātaṁ* - stay with Me; *kuru* - do; *sakhi* - O girlfriend; *sadā* - always; *dānam* - taxation; *etat* - this; *madīyam* - Mine.

"The forest of Vraja is scented by the (ever-increasing) fragrance of lotus and *kuṅkuma* from Your golden limbs, that is carried by the wind from the ocean of fragrance. I cannot think of any proper amount that You can pay Me for this, therefore, O *sakhi*, just pay Me by always staying with Me!" (75)

masṛṇa ghusṛṇa carcā cāru kastūrikodyan
makara kamala vallī patra-bhaṅgādikānām
rati vitaraṇa śūrais tat tad āmoda pūraiḥ
parimalaya mad aṅgaṁ nityam ity eva dānam

masṛṇa - fine; *ghusṛṇa* - vermilion; *carcā* - ointment; *cāru* - beautiful; *kastūrikā* - musk; *udyat* - made of; *makara* - a large fish; *kamala* - lotus; *vallī* - vines; *patra* - leaves; *bhaṅgādikānām* - of pictures; *rati* - love; *vitaraṇa* - distributing; *śūraiḥ* - by the greatest; *tat tad* - those; *āmoda* - pleasure; *pūraiḥ* - with floods; *parimalaya* - please scent; *mad* - My; *aṅgaṁ* - body; *nityam* - always; *iti* - thus; *eva* - certainly; *dānam* - gift.

"You should always scent My body with the stream of fragrance from the leaves, vines, lotus-flowers and Makarī-fishes that are painted on Your body with soft *kuṅkuma* and beautiful musk and that are expert in giving their love." (76)

caraṇa kamala lākṣāśliṣṭa saubhāgya mudrā-
tatir ativalate yā hāriṇī hanta tasyāḥ
mad urasi nakharāgrair ardha-candrān pararddhaṁ
vitara padaka varyān dānam ārād varoru

caraṇa - feet; *kamala* - lotus; *lākṣā* - lac; *āśliṣṭa* -
embraced; *saubhāgya* - good fortune; *mudrā-tatiḥ* - of
marks; *ativalate* - shining; *yā* - Who; *hāriṇī* - charming;
hanta - O!; *tasyāḥ* - Hers; *mad* - My; *urasi* - on the chest;
nakharāgraiḥ - with the tips of the nails; *ardha* - half;
candrāt - from the moon; *pararddhaṁ* - billions; *vitara* -
distribute; *padaka* - medal; *varyān* - excellent; *dānam* - tax-
payment; *ārād* - close by; *varoru* - O nicely thighed girl.

**"O Varoru (nicely thighed girl)! For the auspi-
cious marks on Your lac-anointed footsoles You must
give Me billions of medals with the halfmoon sign (the
emblem of Cupid) on My chest." (77)**

Notes: *atra vilāsa-viśeṣāvasare kara-nakha-*
samarpaṇam eva bhaṅgyā prārthitam With gestures Kṛṣṇa
prays that She may give Him Her nails (scratch Him) during special erotic pastimes.

dhvānair yasya vipakṣa lakṣa
hṛdayotkampādi sampādakair
āvaikuṇṭham ajāṇḍa-pālir atulānandaiḥ pariplāvitā
prītyā tasya ramādi vandita ruteḥ
aubhāgya sad dundubher
dānaṁ kañja maranda sundarataraṁ gānaṁ tavānandade

dhvānaiḥ - with sounds; *yasya* - whose; *vipakṣa (śrī*
candrāvalyādīnāṁ) - enemy; *lakṣa* - 100,000; *hṛdaya* -
heart; *utkampa* - shiver; *ādi* - and others; *sampādakaiḥ* -
establishing; *ā-vaikuṇṭham* - up to Vaikuṇṭha; *ajāṇḍa-* mun-
dane universe; *pāliḥ* - multitudes; *atula* - matchless;

ānandaiḥ - with ecstasy; *pariplāvitā* - inundating; *prītyā* - with love; *tasya* - his; *ramā* - Lakṣmī; *ādi* - beginning with; *vandita* - praised; *ruteḥ* - of the sound; *saubhāgya* - good fortune; *sat* - real; *dundubheḥ* - of the Dundubhi-drum; *dānaṁ* - giving; *kañja* - lotus; *maranda* - honey; *sundarataraṁ* - more beautiful; *gānaṁ* - song; *tava* - Your; *ānandade* - delightful girl.

"O Ānandade (delightful girl)! For the Dundubhi-drum of Your good fortune, whose sounds give lakhs of Your rival-*gopīs* (like Candrāvalī) a heart-attack, that inundate all the universes upto Vaikuṇṭha with peerless ecstasy, and that is praised by all the goddesses, like Lakṣmī-*devī*, You must give Me Your songs, that are sweeter than lotus-honey!" (78)

nāma svasty ayanaṁ yad atra vilasat pīyūṣato'pi priyaṁ
rādheti prathitaṁ samasta jagatī romañca sañcārakam
tasyāmūlyatarasya dānam
aparaṁ yogyaṁ kvacit kiṁ bhavet
tasmād ujjvala keli ratnam atulaṁ rādhe mamādhīyatām

nāma - name; *svastyayanaṁ* - propitious; *yad* - what; *atra* - here; *vilasat* - shining; *pīyūṣataḥ* - than nectar; *api* - even; *priyaṁ* - dear; *rādhā* - Rādhā; *iti* - thus; *prathitam* - famed' *samasta* - complete; *jagatī* - of the world; *romañca* - goosepimples; *sañcārakam* - infuses; *tasya* - his; *amūlyatarasya* - of the priceless; *dānam* - gift; *aparaṁ* - other; *yogyaṁ* - suitable; *kvacit* - somewhere; *kiṁ* - what; *bhavet* -may be; *tasmād* - therefore; *ujjvala* - erotic; *keli* - play; *ratnam* - jewel; *atulaṁ* - peerless; *rādhe* - O Rādhe!; *mama* - My; *ādhīyatām* - must be given.

"Is there any proper amount You can pay Me for this priceless auspicious name 'Rādhā' that is heard in

Vṛndāvana, that is sweeter than nectar and that gives goosepimples of ecstasy to all the worlds? Therefore, O Rādhe, give Me the incomparible playjewel of erotic play!" (79)

dīvyan mati prathita kīrti-tati pragāḍha
citta prageya guṇa geya guṇotkarāṇām
san mauktika pravara hīraka cāru nīla
ratnojjvalad vividha ratna kulāni kāmam

dīvyat (krīḍā vinodī mati) - playing; *mati* - intelligence; *prathita* - known as; *kīrti-tati* - glories; *pragāḍha* - deep; *citta* - heart; *prageya* - glorious; *guṇa* - attributes; *geya* - sung; *guṇotkarāṇām* - of many qualities; *sat* - true; *mauktika* - pearl; *pravara* - best; *hīraka* - diamonds; *cāru* - beautiful; *nīla-ratna* - sapphires; *ujjvalad* - shining; *vividha* - different; *ratna* - gems; *kulāni* - of the multitude; *kāmam* - enough.

"For Your pure (playful) intelligence, Your celebrated fame and Your attributes, that are fit to be glorified by the most qualified and grave people, You must pay Me many beautiful pearls, the best diamonds, beautiful sapphires and other glistening gems." (80)

Notes: *prakarṣeṇa geyaṁ guṇaṁ yāsāṁ tāṁ pragāḍha-citta prageya guṇāḥ umādi ramaṇyaḥ (umādi ramaṇī-vyūha-spṛhaṇīya guṇotkarām iti kārpaṇya pañjikāyām uktatvāt) tābhir api geyaḥ yaḥ guṇānām utkaraḥ* — "Her great glories are sung by grave persons like Umā (Pārvatī) and other goddesses, as is stated by Śrīla Rūpa Gosvāmī in his Kārpaṇya Pañjikā Stotram — "*umādi ramaṇī-vyūha-spṛhaṇīya guṇotkarām*". *atrāsamordhva-gaurava-mādhurya-pūrṇa-mati-kīrti-guṇa-samūhānāṁ tat tad āsvāda-pracurāḥ kalā-vilāsā eva bhaṅgyā prārthitāḥ*

Through gestures Kṛṣṇa prays that Rādhikā will give Him great relish during artful love-making with Her matchless attributes, that are full of intelligence, glory, dignity and sweetness.

mādyan mataṅga gati nindi-gater anaṅga
raṅgasya saṅga vidhaye kila lagnikāyāḥ
tāroru mauktika marāla varālir āli
māṇikya pālir atha te kara cālanānām

mādyat - maddened; *mataṅga* - elephant; *gati* - gait; *nindi* - mocking; *gateḥ* - of the gait; *anaṅga* - Cupid; *raṅgasya* - of the play; *saṅga* - company; *vidhaye* - for the sake of; *kila* - indeed; *lagnikāyāḥ* - of the guarantee; *tārāḥ* - splendid; *uru* - big; *mauktika* - pearls; *marāla* - swans; *vara* - best; *aliḥ* - hosts; *āli* - O girlfriend; *māṇikya* - gem; *pāliḥ* - a host; *atha* - then; *te* - Your; *kara* -hands; *cālanānām* - of the movements.

"O Ali (*sakhi*)! For Your gait, that defeats the charms of an intoxicated elephant's gait and that guarantees Your amorous company to Me, You must give Me swans made of the best big pearls, that shine like the stars, and for the gestures of Your hands You must give Me many jewels. (81)

Notes: *mada matta kari vijayinaḥ tathā muktāmaya marāla gati garima hāriṇaḥ sauṣṭhava bhara paripoṣita sundara gamanasya abhisārādi samaye vibhramādi vaiśiṣṭhya darśanākāṅkṣā sūcitā pūrvārdhe.* In the first half of the verse Kṛṣṇa indicates His desire to see the speciality of Rādhikā's beautiful gait, that defeats the elegance of an intoxicated elephant and a pearly swan, and Her *vibhramālaṅkāra* (in which She dresses topsy-turvy out of eagerness to meet Kṛṣṇa) as She goes on *abhisāra* (love-journey) *uttarārdhe tu vilāsa viśeṣe svāṅge tat kara vāraṇādi rūpa bhoga eva svābhilāṣaḥ* — In the latter half of the verse He desires to enjoy the touch of Her hands, that try to obstruct Him during the erotic pastimes.

āyur yaśo jaya vivardhana randhanodyad
uddāma sausṭhava bharasya tu kalpitaṁ me
kāyastha vartanatayā madhumaṅgalāya
nityaṁ suśaṣkuli sukuṇḍalikādi dānam

āyuḥ - life-span; *yaśaḥ* - fame; *jaya* - victory; *vivardhana* - expanding; *randhana* - cooking; *udyad* - arising; *uddāma* - great; *sausṭhava* - elegance; *bharasya* - of the abundance; *tu* - but; *kalpitaṁ* -considered; *me* - Mine; *kāyastha* - of the scribe; *vartanatayā* - by profession; *madhumaṅgalāya* - to Madhumaṅgala; *nityaṁ* - always; *suśaṣkuli* - nice cakes; *sukuṇḍalika* - sweets; *ādi* - beginning; *dānam* - gift.

"As wages for My scribe Madhumaṅgala and as payment for Your great elegance that arises while You are cooking You must always prepare the best *jilapis*, *lucis* and so on, that increase My health, lifespan, fame and glory." (82)

Notes: *atra randhanāvasare visrasta vasana bhūṣaṇāder hetoh paramojjvalānāvṛtāṅga-śobhā sandarśanam eva svābhilāṣaḥ* Here Kṛṣṇa desires to see Śrī Rādhikā's most brilliantly beautiful shining limbs that are uncovered due to Her endeavours in cooking, that caused Her garments and ornaments to loosen or fall off.

saundarya hrī vinaya paṇḍitatā sugāna
vaidagdhya sad guṇa-tater bhavad āli-vargaḥ
duḥsādhamāna vikṛter lalitā tvad ālī
tvat prīti narma śubha karma-tate viśākhā

saundarya - beauty; *hrī* - bashfulness; *vinaya* - humility; *paṇḍitatā* - erudition; *sugāna* - great singing; *vaidagdhya* - cleverness; *sat* - real; *guṇa-tateḥ* - of attributes; *bhavat* - Your; *āli-vargaḥ* -girlfriends; *duḥsādha* - difficult to accomplish; *māna* - amorous pique; *vikṛteḥ* - of the transformation; *lalitā* - Lalitā; *tvad* - Your; *ālī* - girlfriend; *tvat* - Your; *prīti* - love; *narma* - humorous; *śubha* -auspicious; *karma-tate* - of the actions; *viśākhā* - Viśākhā.

"For Your beauty, shyness, humility, erudition, nice singing, cleverness and other good qualities You must give Me Your girlfriends. For Your pique, which is so hard to soothe, You must give Me Lalitā and for Your loving auspicious, humorous activities You must give Me Viśākhā." (83)

kāntyā'ti nindita ramā śata lakṣa kāntes
tvad vigrahasya bhavati sudatiṣv amūlyā
lakṣmī sahasra śatato'py ati ramya goṣṭha
rāmā śiro varamaṇes tava vigraho'sau

kāntyā - with luster; *ati* - very much; *nindita* - mocked; *ramā* - goddess of fortune; *śata* - hundred; *lakṣa* - 100,000; *kānteḥ* - of the luster; *tvad* - Your; *vigrahasya* - of the form; *bhavati* - Your; *sudatiṣu* - amongst girl with nice teeth; *amūlyā* - priceless; *lakṣmī* - Lakṣmī; *sahasra* - thousand; *śatataḥ* - than a hundred; *api* - even; *ati* - very much; *ramya* - lovely; *goṣṭha* - Vraja; *rāmā* - girls; *śiraḥ* - on the head; *vara* - best; *maṇeḥ* - of the jewel; *tava* - Your; *vigrahaḥ* - form; *asau* - this.

"The luster of Your beautiful form mocks that of millions of goddesses of fortune. For this Your body, which is priceless among all the beautiful girls, is the price! You are the crownjewel of all the *gopīs* of Vraja,

who are again enchanting hundreds of thousands of goddesses of fortune !" (84)

Notes: *atrānyonyopamā - yad uktam alaṅkāra kaustubhe 'viparyāsa upameyopamā dvayoḥ'. tena ca vigraha tadvatyoya bhedenoktatvād ramaṇecchu śata lakṣa-kāminī vijayi kānti-śīlasya vigrahasya vā tat kānti yuktāyāḥ vā nigūḍha sambhogātiśayaḥ parihāsa bhaṅgyā prārthitaḥ yatra gāḍha vilāsa vibhrāntau sampariṣvaktau bāhyāntara saṁvedana rahitau yugala kiśorau paramānanda rasa nimagnau virājatas tamām* — Here is a mutual comparison, which is described in Alaṅkāra Kaustubha as a contrariety between the object of comparison and the standard of comparison. With joking gestures Kṛṣṇa prays for great intimate enjoyment, where deep love enjoyment is manifest. the yugal kiśora forgets all difference between external and internal and remain immersed in the *rasa* of topmost erotic bliss.

tad vākyam ittham adhikaṁ madhuraṁ niśamya
rādhā tiraskṛta sudhā'tula sindhu garvam
utphulla kopa lalita smita narma ramyaṁ
bhaṅgyā lalāpa kuṭilaṁ kuṭilaṁ nirīkṣya

yāsyāmy ahaṁ nahi pathā rata-hiṇḍakena
sandūṣitena nitarāṁ sakhi tena tena
ittham mad uktam api naiva niśamya garvād
ānīya mām iha dadau lalitā kare'sya

tat - this; *vākyam* - words; *ittham* - thus; *adhikaṁ* - greater; *madhuraṁ* - sweet; *niśamya* - having heard; *rādhā* - Rādhā; *tiraskṛta* - rebuking; *sudhā* - nectar; *atula* - matchless; *sindhu* - ocean; *garvam* - pride; *utphulla* - blossomed; *kopa* - anger; *lalita* - lovely (*sukumāratayāṅgānāṁ vinyāsaḥ* - moving the limbs in a tender way); *smita* - smile;

narma - humorous; *ramyaṁ* - charming; *bhaṅgyā* - with gestures; *lalāpa* - speaking; *kuṭilaṁ* - crookedness; *kuṭilaṁ* - the crooked one (Tribhaṅgī Śyāma); *nirīkṣya* - seeing. *yāsyāmi* - I will go; *ahaṁ* - I; *nahi* - not; *pathā* - by this path; *rata-hiṇḍakena* - by a woman-thief; *sandūṣitena* - by polluting; *nitarāṁ* - constantly; *sakhi* - O girlfriend; *tena tena* - by Him; *itthaṁ* - thus; *mad* - My; *uktam* - words; *api* - even; *na* - not; *eva* - certainly; *niśamya* - having heard; *garvād* - out of pride; *ānīya* - bring; *mām* - me; *iha* - here; *dadau* - placed; *lalitā* - Lalitā; *kare* - in the hand; *asya* - His.

"Hearing Śyāma's very sweet words, that destroyed the pride of the sweetness of boundless oceans of nectar, Rādhā looked at this three-fold-bended swain in a crooked way and said with joking gestures, a charming smile and feigned anger: "*Sakhi*! Although I told Lalitā: "O *Sakhi*! I will not proceed on this path polluted by this woman-thief!", she did not listen to Me out of pride and placed Me here into His hands!" (85-86)

Notes: *atra śrī rādhāyāḥ kila kiñcita bhāvodgamo draṣṭavyaḥ. yad uktam ujjvale - garvābhilāṣa rudita smitāsūyā-bhaya-krudhām. saṅkarī-karaṇam harṣād ucyate kila kiñcitam. utphulleti harṣākhya sthāyi-bhāvasya, laliteti svābhilāṣasya kuṭilam ityasūyā garvayoḥ kopa smite tu vyakte; evam anyad dvayam apy unneyam* "Here we see Śrī Rādhā's *kila kiñcita* arising, which is defined as follows in Ujjvala Nīlamaṇi — "When pride, desire, weeping, smiling, envy, fear and anger all combine out of joy it is called *kila kiñcita*." Utphulla indicates the *sthāyibhāva* known as *harṣa*, or joy, and *lalita* means the crookedness of one's own desires, shown through envy, pride and anger in a smile. The same thing goes for the other two.

evaṁ nigadya sahasā saha sā sakhībhir
vāmyena kāmyam api tat kṛta narma śarma

san nindya vandya vadanā vidhunā vrajantī
ruddhā balena vidhunā vidhunā vrajasya

evaṁ - thus; *nigadya* - speaking; *sahasā* - at once; *saha* - with; *sā* - She; *sakhībhiḥ* - with Her friends; *vāmyena* - with opposition; *kāmyam* - desired; *api* - even; *tat* - that; *kṛta* - performed; *narma* -humorous; *śarma* - auspicious; *saṁnindya* - rebuking; *vandya* - praiseworthy; *vadanā* - face (fem.); *vidhunā* - by the moon; *vrajantī* - they go; *ruddhā* - stopped; *balena* - by force; *vidhunā vidhunā vrajasya* - by the moon of Vraja.

Saying this, Śrī Rādhā, whose face is praised by the moon, quickly left with Her girlfriends. Although She wanted to hear Śyāma's auspicious joking words She chastised Him, but that moon of Vraja, Śrī Kṛṣṇa, forcibly stopped Her. (87)

śrutvā mukunda madhura smita sikta narma
marma prabandham atulaṁ kim api smitākṣī
antaḥ sphurat sukha-bharaṁ pracuraṁ ruṣeva
saṁruddhya hṛdyam adhikam lalitā lalāpa

kasyāpi goṣṭha nagare dadhi dugdha dāna
vārtāpi na śruta-carī kim u dṛṣṭa pūrvā
cillābha vargapatinā yad anena sṛṣṭam
etat tu ballabavadhū kula luṇṭhanāya

etasya kṛṣṇa bhujagasya kaṭhora bhogāt
sakhyo yadi svam avituṁ param icchataitat
gatvā vrajendra gṛhiṇī purato yaśo'sya
saṅgīyatāṁ tyajati vaḥ sukhito yathaiṣaḥ

śrutvā - having heard; *mukunda* - Mukunda; *madhura* - sweet; *smita* - smile; *sikta* - sprinkled; *narma* - humorous; *marma* - heart; *prabandham* - words; *atulaṁ* - unrivalled; *kim api* - indescribable; *smita* - smile; *akṣī* - eyes;

antaḥ - inner; *sphurat* - vision; *sukha-bharam* - great happiness; *pracuraṁ* - abundant; *ruṣā* - anger; *iva* - as if; *samruddhya* - checking; *hṛdyam* - pleasant; *adhikam* - greater; *lalitā* - Lalitā; *lalāpa* - prattled. *kasya* - of someone; *api* - even; *goṣṭha* - Vraja; *nagare* - in the town; *dadhi* - yoghurt; *dugdha* - milk; *dāna* - tax; *vārtā* - topics; *api* - even; *na* - not; *śruta-carī* - heard; *kim u* - indeed; *dṛṣṭa* - seen; *pūrvā* - previously; *cillābha* - robbers; *varga* - band; *patinā* - by the boss; *yad* -what; *anena* - by Him; *sṛṣṭam* - created; *etat* - that; *tu* - but; *ballaba-vadhū* - gopīs; *kula* - group; *luṇṭhanāya* - for plundering. *etasya* - of this; *kṛṣṇa* - black; *bhujagasya* - of the snake, the crownjewel of lusty boys, Kṛṣṇa; *kaṭhora* - hard; *bhogāt* - from the coils, or from Kṛṣṇa's hard-core enjoyment; *sakhyaḥ* - O friends!; *yadi* - if; *svam* - himself; *avituṁ* - protecting; *param* - supreme, or proper; *icchatha* - desiring; *etat* - this; *gatvā* - having gone; *vrajendra gṛhiṇī* - Queen Yaśodā; *purataḥ* - before; *yaśaḥ* - glories; *asya* - of Him; *saṅgīyatāṁ* - should be sung; *tyajati* - will abandon; *vaḥ* - us; *sukhitaḥ* - happy; *yathā* - just as; *eṣaḥ* - He.

Although smiling-eyed Lalitā was very happy to hear Śrī Mukunda's incomparibly sweet joking words she checked her great ecstasy and, pretending to be angry, spoke the following sweet words: "We have never heard of anybody levying tax on yoghurt and milk here in Vraja, nor have we ever seen such a person! This dacoit simply made this toll-station here to plunder the *gopīs!* O *Sakhis!* If you really want to protect yourselves from the hard *bhoga* (coils, or enjoyment) of this *Kṛṣṇa bhujaga* (black snake, or Kṛṣṇa, the king of enjoyers), then go to the queen of Vraja and sing His glories to her. Then He will be happy to leave you alone!" (88-90)

Notes: *svābhiyoga-pakṣe tu - kṛṣṇasya kāmamaya-vilāsāvalim āśritya yadi sva rakṣaṇe yuktim kuryāta, tadā yaśodāyāḥ nagarataḥ anyatra vanādau gatvā asya keli-vilāsādi yaśo-rāśim tathā gāyata, yathā tenoddīpitaḥ ayam yuṣmābhiḥ saha yatheccha vihārādikam kurvāṇaḥ sātiśaya sukham anubhavan yuṣmān sva sva gṛhebhyaḥ prerayati.—* Pun: "If you wish to protect yourself and take shelter of Kṛṣṇa's lusty enjoyments, then get out of Yaśodā's town and go to another forest to sing the glories of these lusty pastimes. Thus incited, He will will freely enjoy with You and experience great happiness, after which He sends you back to your own homes."

*rādhā hṛd ākūtam agādham īṣad
vyaṅgena vijñāya mukunda ārāt
pratyekam alpa smitam atra
kṛtvā jagāda bhaṅgyā lalitādikās tāḥ*

*vidyā-cayasya tava sundari tuṅgavidye
pratyekam eva kila lakṣa suvarṇa dakṣam
yat tena tena bhavatī vraja yauvatam taj
jitvā sphuraty anudinam mada darpa dṛptā*

rādhā - Rādhā; *hṛd* - heart; *ākūtam* - intention (to ascertain the taxation on each *sakhī*); *agādham* - deep; *īṣad* - slightly; *vyaṅgena* - with hints; *vijñāya* - learning; *mukunda* - Mukunda; *ārāt* - from a distance; *pratyekam* - each one; *alpa* - slight; *smitam* - smile; *atra* - here; *kṛtvā* - having done; *jagāda* - speaking; *bhaṅgyā* - with gestures; *lalitādikāḥ* - beginning with Lalitā; *tāḥ* - they. *vidyā-cayasya* - amounts of knowledge; *tava* - your; *sundari* - beautiful; *tuṅgavidye* - O Tuṅgavidyā; *pratyekam* - each one; *eva kila* - certainly; *lakṣa* - 100,000; *suvarṇa* - gold; *dakṣam* - expert; *yat* - which; *tena tena* - by that; *bhavatī* - you; *vraja yauvatam* - the young girls of Vraja; *tat* - them;

jitvā - after defeating; *sphurati*- manifest; *anudinaṁ* - every day; *mada darpa* - pride; *dṛptā* - filled.

"Mukunda could understand the innermost feelings in Rādhikā's heart from afar, so He smiled slightly and addressed each of the *gopīs* like Lalitā in a crooked way, saying: "O Beautiful Tuṅgavidye! It is proper for you to give Me a hundred thousand gold coins for each of your branches of knowledge, with which You always proudly defeat the young *gopīs* of Vraja!" (91-92)

Notes: *atrāṅga-pratyaṅgānāṁ sambhoga-lālasā sūcitā* "Here the desire to enjoy each of the limbs is indicated."

> *citre sucitra mṛdu manda vacaḥ prabandho*
> *hṛdyo na kasya tava sundari bhūtale'smin*
> *no cet katham tam avagamya budhaḥ sudhāyāḥ*
> *mādhuryam apy anudinaṁ hi tiraskaroti*

> *asmād amuṣya madhurasya na ko'pi dāna*
> *yogyaḥ padārtha iha bhāvini dṛśyate yat*
> *tasmat idaṁ mṛdula mañjula mṛṣṭa divya*
> *bimbādharāmṛtam idaṁ smita candra gandhī*

citre - O Citre! *sucitra* - very wonderful; *mṛdu manda* - soft; *vacaḥ* - words; *prabandhaḥ* - words; *hṛdyaḥ* - pleasant; *na* - not; *kasya* - whose; *tava* - your; *sundari* - beautiful girl; *bhū* - earth; *tale* - on the surface; *asmin* - in this; *no* - not; *cet* - if; *kathaṁ* - how; *tam* - them; *avagamya* - having known; *budhaḥ* - intelligent; *sudhāyāḥ* - of the nectar; *mādhuryam* - sweetness; *api* - even; *anu-dinaṁ* - every day; *hi* - certainly; *tiraskaroti* - rebukes. *asmāt* - therefore; *amuṣya* - of this; *madhurasya* - of the sweet; *na* - not; *ko'pi* - anything; *dāna* - taxation; *yogyaḥ* - fit; *padārtha* - objects;

iha - here; *bhāvini* - beautiful girl; *dṛśyate* - seen; *yat* - what; *tasmat* - therefore; *idam* - this; *mṛdula* - soft; *mañjula* - lovely; *mṛṣṭa* - rubbed; *divya* - divine; *bimba* - cherry; *adhara* - lips; *amṛtam* - nectar; *idam* - this; *smita* - smile; *candra* - camphor; *gandhī* - fragrant.

"O beautiful Citre! Whose heart does not melt after hearing Your wonderfully gentle and pleasant words? Otherwise why would the learned men who hear these words always criticize the sweetness of nectar? O Bhāvini (beautiful girl)! I cannot find a proper tax for such sweet words in this world, so give Me the nectar of Your lips that are like Bimba-fruits scented with the divine, soft, lovely and spotless camphor of your smile!" (93-94)

prāṇāli campakalate tava vahni tapta
jāmbūnada sphurita campaka kampi kānteḥ
śyāmam mad aṅgam ucitam muditā tayaiva
san mālayā madhurayā kila maṇḍayeti

prāṇāli - heart's friend; *campakalate* - Campakalatā; *tava* - your; *vahni* - fire; *tapta* - molten; *jāmbūnada* - gold; *sphurita* - beautified; *campaka* - Campaka-flowers; *kampi* - trembling; *kānteḥ* -of the lustre; *śyāmam* - dark; *mad* - my; *aṅgam* - body; *ucitam* - fit; *muditā* - gladly; *tayā* - by her; *eva* - certainly; *sat* - real; *mālayā* - by a garland; *madhurayā* - by the sweetness; *kila* - certainly; *maṇḍaya* - decorate; *iti* - thus.

"O Prāṇa-sakhi Campakalate! As payment for your lustre of molten gold, that defeats the luster of trembling Campaka-flowers, you must gladden My bluish limbs by adorning them with this sweet beautiful Campaka-garland (your embrace)!" (95)

yat te mukhasya madhu tan madhurāṅgi narma
karpūra vāsitataraṁ rasa-digdha mugdham
tasyaiva durlabhatarasya paraṁ viśākhe
dānaṁ tvam eva niyatāṁ na paraṁ trilokyām

yat - what; *te* - your; *mukhasya* - of the face; *madhu* - honey; *tat* - that; *madhura* - sweet; *aṅgi* - body; *narma* - humorous; *karpūra* - camphor; *vāsitataraṁ* - scented; *rasa* - flavour; *digdha* - anointed; *mugdham* - charming; *tasya* - his; *eva* - certainly; *durlabhatarasya* - more rare; *paraṁ* - supreme; *viśākhe* - O Viśākhā; *dānaṁ* - donation; *tvam* - you; *eva* - only; *niyatāṁ* - indicated; *na* - not; *paraṁ* -another; *tri* - three; *lokyām* - of the worlds.

"O Madhurāṅgi (sweet-limbed) Viśākhe! You yourself are the tax for the sweet tasty nectar of Your lips, that is scented by the camphor of Your joking words, and that is very precious; there's no other levy imaginable in this world!" (96)

vaidagdhya narma rasa lāsya vilāsa hāsa
saundarya sad guṇa-tater lalite paraṁ te
mānoru śikṣaṇa vicakṣaṇatādi kūṭa
kāṭhinya kauśala parityajanaṁ hi dānam

vaidagdhya - cleverness; *narma* - humour; *rasa* - flavour; *lāsya* - dancing; *vilāsa* - enjoyment; *hāsa* - laughing; *saundarya* - beauty; *sat* - good; *guṇa* - attributes; *tateḥ* - of the multitude; *lalite* - Lalitā!; *paraṁ* - supreme; *te* - your; *māna* - pride; *uru* - great; *śikṣaṇa* - teaching; *vicakṣaṇatā* - expertise; *ādi* - beginning; *kūṭa* - shrewd; *kāṭhinya* - hardness; *kauśala* - expertise; *parityajanaṁ* - renunciation; *hi* - certainly; *dānam* - payment.

"O Lalite! For your supreme cleverness, joking humour, playful dancing, laughter, beauty and all other good qualities you must pay Me by giving up your expert, hard and shrewd instructions on *mana* (pique) to Sri Radhika!" (97)

sudhanidhi sudha bharaih krta vicitra sat kundika
sprha sata visarjaka sphurita madhuri bindukam
tayor vraja vilasinor madhura keli varta sudham
dhayanty api sahasrasah sumukhi naiva trptim labhe

sudhanidhi - nectar ocean; *sudha* - nectar; *bharaih* - by the abundance; *krta* - performed; *vicitra* - wonderful; *sat* - real; *kundika* - big cup; *sprha* - desire; *sata* - hundred; *visarjaka* - abandoning; *sphurita* - manifest; *madhuri* - sweetness; *bindukam* - a drop; *tayoh* - of the both; *vraja vilasinoh* - of the Vraja-enjoyers; *madhura* - sweet; *keli* - play; *varta* - topics; *sudham* - nectar; *dhayanti* - they drink; *api* - even; *sahasrasah* - thousands; *sumukhi* - fair-faced girls; *na* - not; *eva* - certainly; *trptim* - satisfaction; *labhe* - attaining.

"O Sumukhi!", Kundalata said, "Although I drink the sweet nectar of the Vraja Yugala's pastimes, a drop of which removes the desire for the sweetness of big beautiful pots with the essence of the nectar ocean a thousand times, I cannot be satisfied with it, so go on speaking!" (98)

Notes: *kundaliti pathe, sudha pracuryotthita- vividha gabhiravarta sprha-laksanam parityajakam ity-arthah* — When the word *.kundika* is read as *kundali* it means: "Removing lakhs of desires that are like different deep whirlpools that arise from an abundance of nectar"._

tasmat punah punar imam kathayaiva vartam
ity adya kundalataya pratibhasyamane

santoṣa sāgara nimajjana phulla roma
premārdra vāg vidhumukhī sumukhī vabhāṣe

tadā tad uktākhila dāna vastu
jātaṁ niśamyāli-kuleṣu teṣu
hasatsu sarveṣu ca tuṅga-narmā
smitvā sphuṭaṁ vācam uvāca goṣṭhyām

vittāni yāni madhumaṅgala yācitāni
tāny āśu neṣyatha kathaṁ bata durbalāḥ stha
tasmād gṛhāc chakaṭa yūtham ihānayadhvaṁ
śūroṣṭra sad vṛṣabha loka kharāṁś ca bodhum

tasmāt - therefore; *punaḥ punaḥ* - again and again; *imaṁ* - this; *kathaya* - please desribe; *eva* -certainly; *vārtām* - topics; *iti* - thus; *adya* - today; *kundalatayā* - by Kundalatā; *pratibhāṣyamāne* - being replied; *santoṣa* - satisfaction; *sāgara* - ocean; *nimajjana* - immersed; *phulla* - blossoming; *roma* - torso-hairs; *prema* - love; *ardra* - moistened; *vāk* - voice; *vidhu-mukhī* - moonfaced girl; *sumukhī* - fair-faced girl; *vabhāṣe* - spoke. *tadā* - then; *tad* - that; *ukta* - spoken; *akhila* - all; *dāna* - taxation; *vastu* - substance; *jātaṁ* - manifest; *niśamya* - having heard; *ali-kuleṣu* - among the *sakhīs;* *teṣu* - among them; *hasatsu* - amongst the laughing; *sarveṣu* - amongst all; *ca* - and; *tuṅga-narmā* - the humorous, playful Tuṅgavidyā; *smitvā* - having smiled; *sphuṭaṁ* - clearly; *vācam* - words; *uvāca* - spoke; *goṣṭhyām* - to the assembly. *vittāni* - wealth; *yāni* - which; *madhumaṅgala* - O Madhumaṅgala!; *yācitāni* - being begged; *tāni* - this; *āśu* - swiftly; *neṣyatha* - will take; *kathaṁ* - how; *bata* - O!; *durbalāḥ* - weak; *stha* - being; *tasmāt* - therefore; *gṛhāt* - from the house; *śakaṭa* - carts; *yūtham* - host; *iha* - here; *ānayadhvaṁ* - bring; *śūra* - big, strong; *uṣṭra* - camels; *sat* - good; *vṛṣabha* - bulls; *loka* - people; *kharāṁ* - mules; *ca* - and; *bodhum* - to carry.

Hearing this, moon-faced Sumukhī drowned in an ocean of bliss. Her skin erupted with goosepimples as she lovingly continued with faltering voice: "After hearing how Kṛṣṇa ascertained the levy, all the *gopīs* and *gopas* began to laugh. Witty Tuṅgavidyā smiled and openly told the assembly: "O Madhumaṅgala! How will you take all the wealth you asked for with you so quickly? You are all so weak! You'd better bring many carts, big camels, asses, bulls and men from your village to carry all this!" (99-101)

> *tat kṛṣṇa narma lapitaṁ lalitaṁ niśamya*
> *thutkāra kārakam apīndu sudhā pravāhe*
> *ānanda saṁsphurita sāttvika bhāva bhāram*
> *āguṇṭhya vāmya madhura madhurāyatākṣī*

tat - that; *kṛṣṇa* - Kṛṣṇa; *narma* - humorous; *lapitaṁ* - words; *lalitaṁ* - lovely; *niśamya* - having heard; *thutkāra kārakam* - rebuking; *api* - even; *indu* - lunar; *sudhā* - nectar; *pravāhe* - in the stream; *ānanda* - transcendental bliss; *saṁsphurita* - manifested; *sāttvika bhāva* - sāttvika ecstasies; *bhāram* - abundance; *āguṇṭhya* - concealing; *vāmya* - opposition; *madhura madhura* - ever-so-sweet; *āyata* - elongated; *akṣī* - eyes (fem.)

Hearing Kṛṣṇa's charming joking words, that defeated the sweetness of streams of lunar nectar, stubborn, wide- and sweet-eyed Rādhikā concealed the symptoms of ecstasy that appeared on Her body. (102)

> *śrīmad goṣṭha-vaneśvarī rasa-kalā līlojjvalan nāgarī*
> *bhrājad goṣṭha mahendra-nandana*
> *mano māṇikya pāṭaccarī*
> *prodyat puṣpa-dhanuḥ prabandha*
> *vividha vyākāra vāg īśvarī*
> *gāndharvā giridhāriṇā vivadate vāṅ nṛtya vidyādharī*

svāmin nu dāsa vanitā na vayaṁ bhavāmaś
candrāvalir na ca vayaṁ na ca padmikā te
yad gūḍha ghora gahane miṣataḥ karasya
saṁluṇṭhanāya bhavatā bata rakṣitāḥ smaḥ

śrīmad - beautiful; *goṣṭha* - Vraja; *vana* - forest; *īśvarī* - goddess; *rasa* - flavours; *kalā* - arts; *līlā* - pastimes; *ujjvalat* - glistening; *nāgarī* - heroine; *bhrājad* - shining; *goṣṭha* - Vraja; *mahā* - great; *indra* - king; *nandana* - son; *manaḥ* - mind; *māṇikya* - jewel; *pāṭaccarī* - thief (fem.); *pra* - strongly; *udyat* - arising; *puṣpa-* flower; *dhanuḥ* - bow; *prabandha* - words; *vividha* - different kinds; *vyākāra* - explanations; *vāk īśvarī* - Sarasvatī, the goddess of speech; *gāndharvā* - Rādhā; *giridhāriṇā* - with Giridhārī; *vivadate* - quarrel; *vāk* - words; *nṛtya* - dancing; *vidyā-dharī* - expert. *svāmin* - master; *nu* - indeed; *dāsa -vanitā* - slaves (fem.); *na* - not; *vayaṁ* - we; *bhavāmaḥ* - are; *candrāvaliḥ* - Candrāvalī; *na* - not; *ca* - and; *vayaṁ* - we; *na* - not; *ca* - and; *padmikā* - Padmā; *te* - Your; *yat* - that; *gūḍha* - solitary; *ghora* - terrible; *gahane* - in the forest; *miṣataḥ* - on the pretext; *karasya* - of taxation; *saṁluṇṭhanāya* - for robbing; *bhavatā* - by You; *bata* - O!; *rakṣitāḥ smaḥ* - arrest.

Then Gāndharvā, the queen of beautiful Vṛndāvana, the jewel of playful, artistic erotic heroines who steals the jewel of Vrajendra-nandana (Kṛṣṇa)'s mind, who is the expert Sarasvatī who can make Her words dance in such a way that they arouse desire in His heart, began to quarrel with Giridhārī, saying: "O Svāmin! We are not Your slaves, neither are we Candrāvalī or Padmā that You can just arrest us in the terrifying, lonely forest to rob us on the pretext of levying tax on us!" (103-104)

Notes: *svāmin mahā-manmatha-rāja manya, kathā-mātra svāmin vā* The word *svāmin* means the great king Cupid, or a person who is master only in name.

rādhe mudhā na kuru vāda vivāda vṛddhiṁ
jñātvā hitaṁ mad uditaṁ mama dehi dānam
no cen mahā madana eṣa niśamya roṣāt
saṁśāsti vo yadi tadā mama neha doṣaḥ

rādhe - O Rādhe! *mudhā* - vainly; *na* - not; *kuru* - do; *vāda vivāda* - quarrel; *vṛddhiṁ* - expand; *jñātvā* - having known; *hitaṁ* - benefit; *mat* - My; *uditaṁ* - words; *mama* - my; *dehi* - give; *dānam* - taxation; *no* - not; *cet* - if; *mahā* - great; *madana* - Cupid; *eṣa* - this; *niśamya* - having heard; *roṣāt* - out of anger; *saṁśāsti* - punish; *vaḥ* - you; *yadi* - if; *tadā* - then; *mama* - My; *na* - not; *iha* - here; *doṣaḥ* - fault.

Kṛṣṇa replied: "O Rādhe! Don't vainly expand this quarrel! Know that I am telling You this for Your own sake — Pay Me the tax! If the great king Cupid finds out about it he will become very angry and severely punish You, and that won't be My fault!" (105)

mithyaivāyaṁ sṛjati nahi ced dānam etad tato'sau
preyaś candrāvali vara śiraḥ śāpam aṅgīkarotu
smitvā govardhana giridarī gehinī raṅgiṇītthaṁ
vācaṁ lāsyaṁ sakhi vidadhati hāsayamāsa goṣṭhīm

mithyā - false; *eva* - certainly; *ayaṁ* - this Kṛṣṇa; *sṛjati* - created; *nahi* - not; *cet* - if; *dānam* - taxation; *etat* - this; *tataḥ* - then *asau* - He; *preyaḥ* - beloved; *candrāvali* - Candrāvalī; *vara* - greatest; *śiraḥ* - head; *śāpam* - curse; *aṅgīkarotu* - may accept; *smitvā* - having smiled; *govardhana* - Govardhana; *giri* - mountain; *darī* - cave; *gehinī* -

housewife; *raṅgiṇī* - playful; *ittham* - thus; *vācam* - words; *lāsyam* - dancing; *sakhi* - girlfriends; *vidadhati* - causing; *hāsayamāsa* - making laugh; *goṣṭhīm* - the assembly.

All the assembled *sakhīs* laughed when Śrī Rādhikā, the playful queen of the caves of Govardhana Hill, jokingly said: "If He (Kṛṣṇa) falsely erected this tollstation He can accept a curse of His beloved Candrāvalī on His fine head!" (106)

Notes: *anena dāna līlā prasaṅgānte govardhana giri guhāyāṁ bhāvi vilāsaḥ sūcitaḥ* By calling Her *govardhana giridarī gehinī*, Śrīla Raghunātha dāsa Gosvāmī indicates that after the Dāna *līlā* Śrī Rādhikā will enjoy with Kṛṣṇa in the caves of Govardhana Hill.

śuddhā vibhāti ca dhiyā śubhayā viśākhā
vaidagdhya narma nipuṇā bhavad antaraṅgā
tasmāt tayā saha vicārya vicārya kāryaṁ
kuryāḥ pramatta lalitā matim āśu muñca

śuddhā - pure; *vibhāti* - shines; *ca* - and; *dhiyā* - with intelligence; *śubhayā* - auspicious; *viśākhā* - Viśākhā; *vaidagdhya* - cleverness; *narma* - humorous; *nipuṇā* - expert; *bhavad* - Your; *antaraṅgā* - intimate friend; *tasmāt* - therefore; *tayā saha* - with Her; *vicārya* - consider; *vicārya kāryaṁ* - acts to be considered; *kuryāḥ* - act; *pramatta* - inebriated; *lalitā* - Lalitā; *matim* - intelligence; *āśu* - swiftly; *muñca* - abandon.

"This Viśākhā has become pure through her blessed intelligence, she is your intimate friend who is also very expert in clever joking. It's good to consider all the duties with her. Immediately reject the advice of Lalitā's bewildered intelligence!" (107)

dānīndra-candra bhavata stavato yato'haṁ
prāptā sukhaṁ tad iha te'pi sukhāni dātrī
draṣṭuṁ bhavan madhura dhārṣṭya bhujaṅga nṛtyam
utkā'bhimanyu garuḍaṁ tarasā'nayāmi

dānī - tax collectors; *indra* - king; *candra* - moon; *bhavata* - from You; *stavataḥ* - from the praises; *yataḥ* - where; *ahaṁ* - I; *prāptā* - attained; *sukhaṁ* - happiness; *tat* - that; *iha* - here; *te* - to You; *api* - even; *sukhāni* - happiness; *dātrī* - the giver; *draṣṭuṁ* - seeing; *bhavat* - Your; *madhura* -sweet; *dhārṣṭya* - boldness; *bhujaṅga* - snake; *nṛtyam* - dance; *utkā* - eager; *abhimanyu* - Abhimanyu; *garuḍaṁ* - Garuḍa; *tarasā* - quickly; *ānayāmi* - I will bring. *pakṣe* - *madhuraṁ dhārṣṭyaṁ yasya tādṛśasya bhujaṅgasya (kāmukasya) nṛtyaṁ draṣṭum utkā (utkaṇṭhitā) satī abhi-manyuḥ (kopaḥ pakṣe tan nāmaka patiḥ) eva garuḍaḥ tam ānayāmi.*

"O Dānīndra-candra (King of moonlike tax-collectors)! I am pleased with Your praises, so now I am eager to make You very happy by quickly bringing the Abhimanyu Garuḍa (ever-angry snake-eater, or Rādhā's husband) to see the sweet dancing of this shameless snake (Kṛṣṇa, the snake of lust)." (108)

evaṁ nigadya rabhasān mahasā'ti hṛdya
ramyā mahiṣṭha guṇa narmabhir adya sadyaḥ
sadmāni padma-vadanā calituṁ samutkā
ruddhā haṭhena haṭhinā hariṇā viśākhā

evaṁ - thus; *nigadya* - speaking; *rabhasāt* - sudden-ly; *mahasā* - strongly; *ati* - very much; *hṛdya* - pleasant; *ramyā* - charming; *mahiṣṭha* - by the greatest; *guṇa* - attrib-utes; *narmabhiḥ* - with joking; *adya* - now; *sadyaḥ* - at once; *sadmāni* - in the abodes; *padma-vadanā* - lotus faced girl; *calitum* - to go; *samutkā* - eager; *ruddhā* - checked; *haṭhena* - by force; *haṭhinā* - by the rake; *hariṇā* -by Hari; *viśākhā* - Viśākhā.

While saying this, lotus-faced Viśākhā, who is charming because of her delectable beauty, her attributes and her jokes, eagerly started for home, but deceitful Hari forcibly stopped her. (109)

saṁrakṣya dharmam abalāḥ sabalād amuṣmāt
kāmād vimukta kula karma samasta dharmāt
vyāghuṭya yāta gṛham eva satītvavatyaḥ
kiṁ vā ghaṭīr iha samarpya suyāga-śālam

saṁrakṣya - having protected; *dharmam* - religious virtues; *abalāḥ* - weak girls; *sabalād* -violently; *amuṣmāt* - from Him; *kāmād* - out of desire; *vimukta* - abandoned; *kula* - family; *karma* -duties; *samasta* - all; *dharmāt* - from religions; *vyāghuṭya* - turning; *yāta* - you may go; *gṛham* - home; *eva* - certainly; *satītvavatyaḥ* - chaste girls; *kiṁ vā* - or; *ghaṭīḥ* - pots; *iha* - here; *samarpya* - offering; *suyāga* - sacrifice; *śālam* - arena.

"O Weak girls!", Citrā said, "if you want to protect your chastity from this powerful Kṛṣṇa who gave up all family traditions and religious principles out of lust, you'd better quickly go home or go to the sacrificial arena to bring your pots of *ghī* there!" (110)

Notes: *atra svābhilāṣa-pakṣa evaṁ vyākhyeyaṁ —* *satītvam adhikaṁ manyadhve cet, gṛham pratyāvartadhvam — śyāma-prītir adhikā cet, ghaṭṭa-catvare ghṛta-ghaṭīḥ parityajya surata yajña mandiraṁ gacchateti* The explanation of the pun that explains their true desires runs as follows — "If you consider your chastity more important, then go home, but if you love Śyāma more, then leave your pots here at the tax-office and go with Kṛṣṇa to the sacrificial temple of eros."

citroktam ittham adhigatya ruṣeva tuṅga-
vidyā jagāda kuṭila bhruvam unnayantī
jātyā'ti bhītatara gopaka vākya mātrān
mugdhe mudhaiva katham atra vibheṣi citre

rādhā sadā jayati goṣṭha-vanādhi-nāthā
tasyāḥ pracaṇḍa sacivā lalitā ca śūrā
paśyādya tad vana vināśaka go-karārthaṁ
addhvā nayāmi madhumaṅgala bhaṇḍa vipram

citrā - Citrā; *uktam* - words; *ittham* - thus; *adhigatya* - understanding; *ruṣā* - angry; *iva* - as if; *tuṅga-vidyā* - Tuṅgavidyā; *jagāda* - spoke; *kuṭila* - crooked; *bhruvam* - eyebrows; *unnayantī* - raising; *jātyā* - by birth; *ati* - very much; *bhītatara* - frightened; *gopaka* - cowherd; *vākya* - words; *mātrāt* - simply; *mugdhe* - O bewildered girl; *mudhā* - useless; *eva* - certainly; *katham* - who; *atra* - here; *vibheṣi* - you fear; *citre* - O Citrā. *rādhā* - Rādhā; *sadā* - always; *jayati* - victorious; *goṣṭha* - Vraja; *vana* - forest; *ādhināthā* - Queen; *tasyāḥ* - Her; *pracaṇḍa* - powerful; *sacivā* - minister (fem.); *lalitā* - Lalitā; *ca* - and; *śūrā* - powerful; *paśya* - look!; *adya* - now; *tat* - her; *vana* - forest; *vināśaka* - destroyer; *go* - cows; *kara* - taxation; *arthaṁ* - for the sake of; *baddhvā* - having bound; *nayāmi* - I shall lead; *madhu-maṅgala* - Madhumaṅgala; *bhaṇḍa* - clown; *vipram* - brāhmaṇa.

Hearing this, Tuṅgavidyā frowned her eyebrows and said, as if angry: "Citre! You're so stupid! Are you so afraid simply by hearing such words from a born coward like this cowherdboy? The queen of Vṛndāvana

Śrī Rādhā is always victorious and Her prime minister Lalitā is very powerful. Just see! I'm binding up this clownish *brāhmaṇa* Madhumaṅgala as a tax for all the damage the cows have made in the forest!" (111-112)

śrutvā tadīya vacanaṁ madhumaṅgalaṁ taṁ
bhītyā tad ātma savidhe subalādi madhye
saṅkucya tatra cakitam cakitaṁ vasantaṁ
caṇḍaṁ jagāda vihasan sakhi kṛṣṇa candraḥ

mā bhair mahā kṣiti surottama mad vidhasya
sākṣād amuṣya narasiṁhavarasya dṛṣṭyā
caṇḍī pracaṇḍa lalitā'pi ca tuṅgavidyā
sā bhairavī drutam apaiṣyati vītavastrā

śrutvā - having heard; *tadīya* - her; *vacanaṁ* - words; *madhumaṅgalaṁ* - Madhumaṅgala; *taṁ* - him; *bhītyā* - afraid; *tat* - that; *ātma* - self; *savidhe* - in the vicinity; *subalādi* - starting with Subala; *madhye* - in the middle; *saṅkucya* - shrinking; *tatra* - there; *cakitaṁ cakitaṁ* - startled, scared; *vasantaṁ* - remaining; *caṇḍaṁ* - powerful; *jagāda* - said; *vihasan* - laughing; *sakhi* - O friend; *kṛṣṇa candraḥ* - moonlike Kṛṣṇa. *mā* - do not; *bhaiḥ* - fear; *mahā* - great; *kṣiti* - earth; *surottama* - best of gods (*brāhmaṇa*); *mat* - my; *vidhasya* - of the sort; *sākṣād* - directly; *amuṣya* - of this; *narasiṁha* - Narasiṁha; *varasya* - of the best; *dṛṣṭyā* - by seeing; *caṇḍī* - goddess Caṇḍī; *pracaṇḍa* - powerful; *lalitā* - Lalitā; *api* - even; *ca* - and; *tuṅgavidyā* - Tuṅgavidyā; *sā* - she; *bhairavī* - fearsome; *drutam* -quickly; *apaiṣyati* - departing; *vīta* - losing; *vastrā* - garments.

"O *sakhi* Kundalate!", Sumukhī continued, "Hearing these words, Madhumaṅgala fearfully went up to Kṛṣṇa and shyly hid himself between Subala and the other boys, terrified. Seeing this, Śrī Kṛṣṇacandra

laughed loudly and said (sarcastically): "O great *brāhmaṇa*! Don't be afraid! Seeing a Supreme Lord Nṛsiṁha like Me, the Caṇḍī-like (hot-tempered) Lalitā and the Bhairavī-like Tuṅgavidyā will be stripped and they will quickly and fearfully run off !" (113-114)

Note: Caṇḍī and Bhairavī are two man-hating goddesses.

tūrṇaṁ hiraṇyakaśipuṁ bhagavān nṛsiṁha
candrāvalī kaṭu-kucaṁ nakharair vidarya
prahlādam ullasitam āśu kuru tvam ityā-
karṇaiṣa valgu lalitā lapitaṁ jahāsa

tūrṇaṁ - quickly; *hiraṇyakaśipuṁ* - Hiraṇyakaśipu; *bhagavān* - Lord; *nṛsiṁha* - Nṛsiṁha; *candrāvalī* - Candravalī; *kaṭu* - hard; *kucaṁ* - breasts; *nakharaiḥ* - with the nails; *vidarya* - pierce; *prahlādam* - Prahlāda; *ullasitam* - delight; *āśu* - quickly; *kuru* - do; *tvam* - You; *iti* - thus; *ākarṇa* - hearing; *eṣa* - thus; *valgu* - charming; *lalitā* - Lalitā; *lapitaṁ* - words; *jahāsa* - laughed.

Kṛṣṇa laughed when He heard Lalitā say the following charming words: "O Lord Nṛsiṁhadeva! Quickly rip Candrāvalī's hard, Hiraṇyakaśipu-like breasts and delight Your great devotee Prahlāda!" (115)

ced gantum icchasi sakhī nikareṇa sārdhaṁ
rādhe samṛddha dhana bhūṣaṇa lobhatas tvam
tad gaccha kintu laliteha mamāccha kacche
saṁrakṣyatāṁ prati-nidhiḥ punar eṣi yāvat

cet - if; *gantum* - going; *icchasi* - you desire; *sakhī nikareṇa sārdhaṁ* - with the girlfriends; *rādhe* - O Rādhe!; *samṛddha* - increased; *dhana* - wealth; *bhūṣaṇa* - ornaments; *lobhataḥ* - out of greed; *tvam* - you; *tat* - that; *gac-cha* - go; *kintu* - but; *lalitā* - Lalitā; *iha* - here; *mama* - My; *āccha* -pure; *kacche* - in the presence, or (*vastrāñcale vā*) in the fold of My garment; *saṁrakṣyatām* - keeping; *prati-nidhiḥ* - guarantee; *punaḥ* - again; *eṣi* - coming; *yāvat* - until.

Kṛṣṇa said: "O Rādhe! If You and Your girl-friends want to go to this sacrifice out of greed for an increase of wealth and ornaments, then go, but then I will keep Lalitā here in My holy presence (or in the fold of My garment) as a down payment until you return!" (116)

pāpena kena mahatā rata-hiṇḍakena
haste tavaiva vidhinā bata pātitāḥ smaḥ
kintvadya paśya tarasā vacasāṁ tavaiṣāṁ
śāstiṁ prasiddha lalitā dadatī kilāsmi

pāpena - by a sin; *kena* - by what; *mahatā* - great; *rata-hiṇḍakena* - by a woman-thief; *haste* - in the hand; *tava* - Your; *eva* - certainly; *vidhinā* - by fate; *bata* - O!; *pātitāḥ smaḥ* - fallen; *kintu* - but; *adya* - now; *paśya* - look; *tarasā* - quickly; *vacasāṁ* - words; *tava* - Your; *eṣāṁ* - this; *śāstiṁ* - order; *prasiddha* - famous; *lalitā* - Lalitā; *dadatī* - gives; *kila* - certainly; *asmi* - I am.

"O woman thief!", Rādhā replied, "Due to what great sin I committed in the past has Fate now placed Me in Your hands? But now You will see that famous Lalitā will very quickly stifle all Your foul words!" (117)

iti taṁ pratibhāṣya karkaśaṁ lalitā roṣa kaṣāya ruṣitā
nikaṭe kapaṭaiḥ sakhīgaṇān
avadat sundari sā rasonmadā

āryām ihānayatu tūrṇam itā sudevī
citrā'cireṇa kuṭilāṁ jaṭilāṁ saputrām
vṛndottamaṁ sapadi yajñika vipram ekam
ālokituṁ naṭanam asya naṭendra bhartuḥ

iti - thus; *taṁ* - him; *pratibhāṣya* - answer; *karkaśaṁ* - harsh; *lalitā* - Lalitā; *roṣa* - anger; *kaṣāya* - reddened; *ruṣitā* - with anger; *nikaṭe* - close by; *kapaṭaiḥ* - with crooked words; *sakhīgaṇān* -to the girlfriends; *avadat* - said; *sundari* - O beautiful girl; *sā* - she; *rasa* - with the flavour; *unmadā* -inebriated. *āryām* - Queen Yaśodā; *iha* - here; *ānayatu* - may bring; *tūrṇam* - quickly; *itā* - gone; *sudevī* - Sudevī; *citrā* - Citrā; *acireṇa* - swiftly; *kuṭilāṁ* - Kuṭilā; *jaṭilāṁ* - Jaṭilā; *sa* - with; *putrām* - son Abhimanyu; *vṛndā* - Vṛndā; *uttamaṁ* - the greatest; *sapadi* - quickly; *yajñika* - sacrificing; *vipram* -brāhmaṇa; *ekam* - one; *ālokituṁ* - witness; *naṭanam* - dancing; *asya* - this; *naṭendra bhartuḥ* - the king of dancers.

"O Beautiful one!", Sumukhī continued, "When Lalitā heard these harsh words she became red of anger, and intoxicated by *rasa* she spoke the following crooked words to her nearby girlfriends: "Sudevī should quickly get the noble Yaśodā here, Citrā should quickly bring Jaṭilā here with Kuṭilā and Abhimanyu, and Vṛndā should quickly bring one sacrificing *brāhmaṇa*. If they come here they can all see the dancing of this crownjewel of dancers (Kṛṣṇa's naughty behaviour)." (118-119)

itthaṁ tayā lalitayā lapitaṁ saroṣam
ākarṇya goṣṭha ramaṇī dhṛta citta vṛttiḥ
īṣad vihasya dara vīkṣya ca rādhikāṁ tāṁ
saṁvyājahāra ruciraṁ sakhi goṣṭha candraḥ

garvād yasya madīya dānam aniśaṁ
yuṣmābhir ullaṅghyate

manye'ham ca tṛṇāya naiva kuṭile dānair alam tasya vaḥ
paśyādyaiva tad eva navya vikasat tāruṇya ratna mayā
vakṣoje paribhūya śūralalitām rādhe'dhunā luṇṭhyate

    ittham - thus; *tayā* - by her; *lalitayā* - by Lalita; *lapitam* - speaking; *saroṣam* - with anger; *ākarṇya* - hearing; *goṣṭha* - Vraja; *ramaṇī* - woman; *dhṛta* - holding; *citta* - mind; *vṛttiḥ* - activities; *īṣad* - slightly; *vihasya* - smiling; *dara* - slightly; *vīkṣya* - seeing; *ca* - and; *rādhikām* - at Rādhikā; *tām* - Her; *saṁvyājahāra* - spoke; *ruciram* - charming; *sakhi* - O friend; *goṣṭha* - of Vraja; *candraḥ* - the moon. *garvāt* - out of pride; *yasya* - whose (jewels of youth); *madīya* - my; *dānam* - taxation; *aniśam* - day and night; *yuṣmābhiḥ* - by you; *ullaṅghyate* - is violated; *manye* - considering; *aham* - I; *ca* - and; *tṛṇāya* - unto the grass; *na* - not; *eva* - certainly; *kuṭile* - O crooked girl; *dānaiḥ* - through taxation; *alam* - uselessly; *tasya* - his; *vaḥ* - you; *paśya* - look; *adya* - now; *eva* - certainly; *tat* - that; *eva* - certainly; *navya* - new; *vikasat* - blossoming; *tāruṇya* - of youth; *ratna* - jewels; *mayā* - by me; *vakṣoje* - on the breast; *paribhūya* - having defeated; *śūra* - powerful; *lalitām* - Lalitā; *rādhe* - O Rādhā; *adhunā* - now; *luṇṭhyate* - is plundered.

    "O Sakhi! Hearing Lalita's angry words Kṛṣṇa, the moon of Vraja, who desired the Vraja-*gopis*, smiled slightly and looked at Rādhikā for a moment, fixing His mind on Her. Then again He sweetly said: "O Crooked Rādhe! There's no more need for taxing those things (Your youthful beauty) of which You were always so proud that You dared to ignore My taxation and to consider Me to be as insignificant as a piece of straw - but look now: defeating the powerful Lalitā I plundered the newly sprouted jewels of youth from Your breasts!" (120-121)

ity ālapya smara vilasitaiḥ spraṣṭum utke mukunde
bhītyevaitās tata ita uta smera vaktrāravindāḥ
krūraṁ tiryaṅ nayana naṭanaiḥ śaśvad ālokayantyaḥ
premāndhas taṁ priyasakhi rasenāpasasruḥ samantāt

iti - thus; *ālapya* - speaking; *smara* - erotic; *vila-sitaiḥ* - with playful gestures; *spraṣṭum* - touching; *utke* - eager; *mukunde* - in Mukunda; *bhītyā* - with fear; *eva* - certainly; *etāḥ* - they; *tata* - then; *itaḥ* - therefore; *uta* - indeed; *smera* - smiling; *vaktra* - faces; *aravindāḥ* - lotusflowers; *krūraṁ* - cruel; *tiryak* - crooked; *nayana* - eyes; *naṭanaiḥ* - with dancing; *śaśvat* - repeatedly; *ālokayantyaḥ* -gazing; *prema* - love; *andhaḥ* - blind; *taṁ* - Him; *priya* - dear; *sakhi* - girlfriend; *rasena* - with flavours; *apasasruḥ* - dispersed; *samantāt* - in all directions.

"O *Sakhi*! After saying this, Mukunda became eager to touch the *gopīs* with playful erotic gestures and with smiling lotuslike faces and dancing cruel eyes they dispersed in all directions from Kṛṣṇa, blinded by love and fear!" (122)

nityaṁ rājānvati janapade divya gavyopahārair
yātāyātaṁ vidadhati janā goṣṭhataḥ koṭi saṅkhyāḥ
naitebhyaḥ kiṁ spṛhayati bhavān dānam ādātum etat
satyaṁ te ced vraja-giri-vane ghaṭṭa paṭṭādhipatyam

nityaṁ - always; *rājānvati-* protected by the righteous king Nanda; *janapade* - in this area; *divya* - pure; *gavya* - dairy products; *upahāraiḥ* - with donations; *yātāyātaṁ* - going and coming; *vidadhati* - performing; *janā* - people; *goṣṭhataḥ* - from Vraja; *koṭi* - millions; *saṅkhyāḥ* - in number; *na* - not; *etebhyaḥ* - from them; *kiṁ* - what; *spṛhayati* - desire; *bhavān* - You; *dānam* - toll; *ādātum* - to collect; *etat* - this; *satyaṁ* - true; *te* - Your; *cet*

- if; *vràja-* Vraja; *giri* - mountains; *vane* - in the forest; *ghaṭṭa paṭṭa* - of the toll-station; *ādhipatyam* - sovereignty.

Śrī Rādhikā said: "Under the protection of the righteous Nanda Mahārāja millions of people always come and go from Vraja to bring donations of pure *ghī* to sacrifices! If You are the tax-collector of all the forests and mountains of Vraja, then why don't You tax them too?" (123)

iti prakaṭa rādhikā vacanam ākalayya prabhur
naṭan nayana bhaṅgībhir niṭilam īṣad uccālayan
aśeṣa rasikāgraṇīḥ sukhabhareṇa rājyan manās
tathāpi bahir uddhasann iva jagāda gāndharvikām

anyebhyo'pi pramada madhunā matta cittaḥ śṛṇudhvaṁ
gṛhnāmy etan niravadhi mudā rāja-mārge vrajadbhyaḥ
yūyaṁ tyaktvā tad anudivasaṁ gūḍham atrāvrajantī
tyevaṁ śrutvā nijacara mukhān manmathaś cakravartī

mām ānīyāntikam atha ruṣā bhartsayitvā samantād
ugraṁ datvā śapatham aham āśikṣitas tena śaśvat
tūrṇaṁ gacchan tvam iha sagaṇo ghaṭṭa vidhvaṁsinīs tā
vadhvā śāstiṁ sapadi vidadhan mat puraḥ prāpayeti

iti - thus; *prakaṭa* - manifest; *rādhikā* - Rādhikā; *vacanam* - words; *ākalayya* - having heard; *prabhuḥ - aghaṭana-ghaṭana paṭuḥ* - the Lord, who can do the impossible; *naṭat* - dancing; *nayana* -eyes; *bhaṅgībhiḥ* - with gestures; *niṭilam* - the forehead; *īṣad* - slightly; *uccālayan* - rising; *aśeṣa* - endless; *rasika* - relisher; *agraṇīḥ* - the crown jewel; *sukha-bhareṇa* - with great bliss; *rājyat* - shining; *manāḥ* - mind; *tathāpi* - still; *bahiḥ* - outside; *uddhasann* - laughing; *iva* - as if; *jagāda* - spoke; *gāndharvikām* - to Rādhā. *anyebhyaḥ* - than others; *api* - even; *pramada* - of happiness; *madhunā* - by the honey; *matta* - inebriated; *cittaḥ* - mind; *śṛṇudhvam* - hear me; *gṛhṇāmi* - I take; *etat* - this; *niravadhi* - relentlessly; *mudā* - joyfully; *rāja-mārge* - on the royal road; *vrajadbhyaḥ* - from the travellers; *yūyam* - you (plural); *tyaktvā* - having abandoned; *tat* - this; *anu* - every; *divasam* - day; *gūḍham* - secretly; *atra* - here; *āvrajanti* - come; *iti* - thus; *evam* - thus; *śrutvā* - having heard; *nija* - own; *cara* - servants; *mukhāt* - from the mouth; *manmathaḥ* - Cupid; *cakravartī* - the great king. *mām* - Me; *ānīya* - bringing; *antikam* - close by; *atha* - then; *ruṣā* - anger; *bhartsayitvā* - chastising; *samantād* - everywhere; *ugram* - terrible; *datvā* - having given; *śapatham* - curse; *aham* - I; *āśikṣitaḥ* - taught; *tena* - by him; *śaśvat* - constantly; *tūrṇam* - quickly; *gacchan* - going; *tvam* - You; *iha* - here; *saganaḥ* - with associates; *ghaṭṭa* - the toll; *vidhvaṁsinīḥ* - destroying; *tā* - they; *vadhvā* - having bound; *śāstim* - punishment; *sapadi* - suddenly; *vidadhan* - making; *mat* - me; *puraḥ* - before; *prāpaya* - bring; *iti* - thus.

Hearing this public statement, the crownjewel of *rasikas* (relishers) Śrī Kṛṣṇa (who can accomplish the impossible) slightly raised His eyebrows with the dancing gestures of His eyes, loudly laughed and told Gāndharvikā: "O Weak girls that are intoxicated by the honey of bliss! Listen, I'm also always blissfully taxing other people that come down this main road, but You are trying to avoid Me by secretly going down this path. When king Cupid heard this from his spies he called Me and angrily rebuked Me, ordering Me: "Quickly go there with your assistents, bind these girls, that are ruining my taxation, up and bring them before Me for punishment!" (124-126)

*tataḥ kumbhān samuttarya nirvṛtā api tāḥ param
nirviṇṇā iva bhaṅgyaiva viviśur bhū-bhṛtas tale*

tataḥ - then; *kumbhān* - the pots; *samuttarya* - lifting; *nirvṛtā* - ecstatic; *api* - even; *tāḥ* - they; *param* - greatly; *nirviṇṇā* - morose; *iva* - as if; *bhaṅgyā* - with gestures; *eva* - certainly; *viviśuḥ* - sat down; *bhū-bhṛtaḥ* - mountain; *tale* - on the base.

Then the *gopīs*, who were actually very happy, brought down their jugs as if unhappy and sat down on the base of Govardhana Hill. (127)

ityādi tan madhura keli vilāsa vārtā
pīyūṣam ullasita karṇa puṭair nipīya
ānandataḥ pulaka gadgada rāva cāru
saṁvyājahāra mṛdu kundalatā tadānīm
śaśvat tayor atula keli kalāmṛtāni
kāmaṁ dhayanty api manāg api naimi tṛptim
tasmāt punaḥ kathaya sundari kiṁ tato'bhūd
etat tad uktam adhigamya jagāda sā ca

iti - thus; *ādi* - beginning; *tat* - that; *madhura* - sweet; *keli* - play; *vilāsa* - enjoyments; *vārtā* -topics; *pīyūṣam* - nectar; *ullasita* - filled with the nectar of happiness; *karṇa* - ear; *puṭaiḥ* - by the cups; *nipīya* - having drunk; *ānandataḥ* - from bliss; *pulaka* - hairs standing up; *gadgada* - stuttering voice; *rāva* - sounds; *cāru* - beautiful; *saṁvyājahāra* - spoke; *mṛdu* - softly; *kundalatā* - Kundalatā; *tadānīm* -then. *śaśvat* - constantly; *tayoḥ* - of both; *atula* - matchless; *keli* - play; *kalā* - arts; *amṛtāni* - nectar; *kāmaṁ* - sufficiently; *dhayanti* - they drink; *api* - even; *manāk* - slightly; *api* - even; *na* - not; *emi* - I attain; *tṛptim* - satisfaction; *tasmāt* - therefore; *punaḥ* - again; *kathaya* - speak!; *sundari* - O beautiful girl; *kiṁ* - what; *tataḥ* - then; *abhūd* - became; *etat* - this; *tat* - that; *uktam* - said; *adhigamya* - having understood; *jagāda* - spoke; *sā* - she; *ca* - also.

Drinking the nectar-sweet story of the playful enjoyments of Kṛṣṇa and the *gopīs* through the delighted cups of her ears, Kundalatā spoke with a sweet soft and faltering voice, her hair standing up in ecstasy — "Even though I always drink the nectarean, matchless stories of the Rasika Yugala (the romantic couple Rādhā-Kṛṣṇa) I'm not even slightly satisfied. Therefore, O beautiful one, tell me more, what happened then?" (128-129)

śrutvā tayor dayita dāna-vihāra vārtām
ārtā tad īkṣitum alakṣitam āgatotkā
nāndīmukhī nibhṛta kuñja-gṛhe praviṣṭā
dṛṣṭvā'dbhutaṁ sadasi sā'dbhutam ājagāma

tāṁ vīkṣya tatra sakalāḥ parirabhya kāmam
āmoditaḥ kathitavatya itaḥ sva-vṛttam
kṛṣṇo'pi tal labhanam āśu vihasya śāsyam
āśaṁsya dāna vivṛtaṁ kathayāṁ vabhūva

śrutvā - having heard; *tayoḥ* - of them both; *dayita* - beloved; *dāna-vihāra* - Dāna-pastime; *vārtām* - topic; *ārtā* - afflicted; *tat* - that; *īkṣitum* - seeing; *alakṣitam* - unnoticed; *āgata* - coming; *utkā* - eager; *nāndīmukhī* - Nāndīmukhī; *nibhṛta* - solitary; *kuñja* - bower; *gṛhe* - house; *praviṣṭā* - entered; *dṛṣṭvā* - having seen; *adbhutaṁ* - wonderful; *sadasi* - in the assembly; *sā* - she; *adbhutam* - wonder; *ājagāma* - attained. *tāṁ* - her; *vīkṣya* - seeing; *tatra* - there; *sakalāḥ* - all; *parirabhya* - embracing; *kāmam* - sufficiently; *āmoditaḥ* - delighted; *kathitavatya* - narrated; *itaḥ* - then; *sva* - His; *vṛttam* - activity; *kṛṣṇaḥ* - Kṛṣṇa *api* - even; *tat* - that; *labhanam* - *āgamanam ityarthaḥ* — means here 'arrival'; *āśu* - quickly; *vihasya* - smiling; *śāsyam* - glorious; *āśaṁsya* - praising; *dāna* - taxation; *vivṛtaṁ* - elaboration; *kathayāṁ* - narrated; *vabhūva* - became.

Hearing this, Sumukhī said: "Nāndīmukhī, hearing that the Dāna *līlā* was going on, became very eager to see it and secretly went there, entering a solitary *kuñja*-cottage. After she witnessed this wonderful pastime she joined the assembled *gopīs,* who blissfully embraced her and told her everything that had happened. Kṛṣṇa then praised her for coming exactly in time and smilingly told her His version of the story. (130-131)

smitvā rādhām athodvīkṣya muditāṁ rasa vihvalām
sānandaṁ paramānandaṁ mukundaṁ nijagāda sā

dāninn adbhuta vastūnāṁ śrutvā dānam ihādbhutam
tad vākyam anvabhāvīti jīvādbhiḥ kiṁ na dṛśyate

smitvā - having smiled; *rādhām* - Rādhā; *atha* - then; *udvīkṣya* - seeing; *muditām* - happy; *rasa* - flavour; *vihvalām* - overwhelmed; *sa* - with; *ānandaṁ* - bliss; *paramānandaṁ* - supreme bliss; *mukundaṁ* - to Mukunda; *nijagāda* - spoke; *sā* - she. *dāninn* - O tax-collector!; *adbhuta* - wonderful; *vastūnāṁ* - of the objects; *śrutvā* - having heard; *dānam* - taxation; *iha* - here; *adbhutam* - wonderful; *tat* - his; *vākyam* - words; *anvabhāvi* - understanding; *iti* - thus; *jīvādbhiḥ* - by the living beings; *kiṁ* -what; *na* - not; *dṛśyate* - is seen.

Nāndīmukhī smiled when she saw Śrī Rādhā overwhelmed with happiness and blissfully told the most joyful Mukunda: "O Dānī (Tollcollector)! I heard what wonderful things You taxed from the *gopīs* and now I practically experienced the saying 'What cannot be seen by a living entity?' myself!" (132-133)

kulīnā vratinīr etā rahaḥ saṁrakṣatas tava
apakīrtir alaṁ vīra bhavitā gokule pure

kṛtaṁ kartavyam atraiva tad alaṁ narma-khelay samūhya
muñca muñcaitaḥ satraṁ gacchantu satvaram

kulīnā - to the family; *vratinīḥ* - dedicated; *etā* - they; *rahaḥ* - solitude; *saṁrakṣataḥ* - arrested; *tava* - you; *apakīrtiḥ* - infamy; *alaṁ* - greatly; *vīra* - O hero!; *bhavitā* - will be; *gokule pure* - in the abode of Gokula. *kṛtaṁ* - done; *kartavyam* - duties; *atra* - here; *eva* - certainly; *tat* - that; *alaṁ* - useless; *narma-khelayā* - with humorous games; *samūhya* - understanding My words; *muñca muñca* - release; *etāḥ* - them; *satraṁ* - sacrifice; *gacchantu* - let them go; *satvaram* - quickly.

"O Hero! These girls are housewives under a vow! If You keep them here in a lonely place You will get a very bad reputation here in Gokula! Your work is done, there is no more need of joking play. Knowing this fully, let them go, let them go! Let them quickly go to the sacrificial arena!" (134-135)

Notes: *svābhiyoga-pakṣe — narma-rasena vṛthā samayaṁ na yāpayitvā mad vākyasya svārasyaṁ jñātvā etāḥ tathā kṛtvā muñca yathā śīghram eva surata yajña-sadanaṁ gaccheyur iti bhāvaḥ* Pun: "Don't vainly waste anymore time with this joking! After properly understanding the savour of My words, let them give up all activities here and let them quickly proceed to the arena of Cupid's sacrifice!"

sarvāṅgānām upari lasatā laṅgimenottamāṅge-
nāpi ślāghyaṁ mukha-vidhum imā dyotayantyo'pi dhūrtāḥ
tasmān nīcair hṛdayam api yan nābhim ācchadayeṣur
yatnair baddhas tad iha bhavitā ko'py apūrvaḥ padārthaḥ

tasmāt pūrvaṁ nibhṛtam anayā sthāna yugmaṁ prakāśya
prāyaḥ satyaṁ bhavati nahi vā kāryatāṁ tat pratītiḥ
no ced etad vivṛtim acirāt sūcakāt saṁniśamya
kruddho'smākaṁ madana nṛ-patir daṇḍam uccair vidhātā

sarva - all; *aṅgānām* - of the limbs; *upari* - above; *lasatā* - shining; *laṅgimena* - by the charming; *uttamāṅgena* - by the head; *api* - even; *ślāghyaṁ* - praiseworthy; *mukha* - face; *vidhum* - moon; *imā* - these; *dyotayantyaḥ* - illuminating; *api* - even; *dhūrtāḥ* - rascals; *tasmāt* - from the face; *nīcaiḥ* - by the low; *hṛdayam* - heart; *api* - even; *yat* - which; *nābhim* - navel; *ācchadayeṣuḥ* - among the coverings; *yatnaiḥ* - with endeavours; *baddhaḥ* - bound; *tat* - that; *iha* - here; *bhavitā* - will be; *ko'pi* - indescribable; *apūrvaḥ* - wonderful; *padārthaḥ* - items. *tasmāt* - therefore; *pūrvaṁ* - before; *nibhṛtam* - in private; *anayā* - by Her; *sthāna* - place; *yugmaṁ* - pair; *prakāśya* - manifest; *prāyaḥ* -usually; *satyaṁ* - truth; *bhavati* - is; *nahi* - not; *vā* - or; *karyatāṁ* - may be done; *tat* - this; *pratītiḥ* - faith; *na* - not; *cet* - if; *etad* - this; *vivṛtim* - uncovering; *acirāt* - quickly; *sūcakāt* - from the spy; *saṁniśamya* - having heard; *kruddhaḥ* - anger; *asmākaṁ* - of us; *madana* - Cupid; *nṛ-patiḥ* - King; *daṇḍam* - punishment; *uccaiḥ* - highly; *vidhātā* - will give.

Kṛṣṇa replied: "The moon-like faces of these shameless *gopīs* are praiseworthy even for all the faces that crown other bodies, and the *gopīs* revealed them, but the chests and navels under these *gopīs'* faces must be carefully concealing some more indescribably wonderful items! Let Me therefore first uncover these two places to see if I was right or wrong, otherwise king Cupid will hear about it from the mouth of his spy and he will become angry and severely punish Me!" (136-137)

guptīkartuṁ tad api paramaṁ vastu yat tu tvayā'haṁ
prārthya bhaṅgyā sumati lalite dātum uktvā tad ardham
etat kiṁ syād yad iha vicarel lekhakaḥ sācako'sau
rājñaḥ preyan parama matimān ujjvalaḥ prekṣako'pi

anviṣyadbhyāṁ niravadhi mama
cchidramābhyāṁ tad agre
vyājād etan nibhṛta vivṛtau jñāpitāyām avaśyam
tīvro'tuccair madana nṛpatir mām itas tvādṛśībhiḥ
sārdhaṁ baddhvā nibhṛta tamasi kṣepsyati drāg guhāntaḥ

guptīkartuṁ - hiding; *tat* - that; *api* - even; *paramaṁ* - supreme; *vastu* - substance; *yat* - what; *tu* - but; *tvayā* - by You; *ahaṁ* - I; *prārthya* - was requested; *bhaṅgyā* - through hints; *sumati lalite* - O intelligent Lalitā; *dātum* - giving; *uktvā* - having said; *tat* - that; *ardham* - half; *etat* - this; *kiṁ* - what; *syād* - may be; *yat* - what; *iha* - here; *vicaret* - may act; *lekhakaḥ* - scribe; *sūcakaḥ* - spy; *asau* - he; *rājñaḥ* - of the king; *preyan* - beloved; *parama* - most; *matimān* - intelligent; *ujjvalaḥ* - Ujjvala, Kṛṣṇa's friend; *prekṣaka* - inspector; *api* - even; *anviṣyadbhyāṁ* - searching; *niravadhi* - without limit; *mama* - my; *cchidram* - fault; *ābhyāṁ* - of both inspector and spy; *tad* - of them; *agre* - before; *vyājād* -on some pretext; *etat* - this; *nibhṛta* - solitary; *vivṛtau* - revealing; *jñāpitāyām* - in the revelation; *avaśyam* - inevitably; *tīvrah* - severely; *atuccaiḥ* - great; *madana* - Cupid; *nṛ-patiḥ* - the king; *mām* -me; *itaḥ* - then; *tvādṛśībhiḥ* - by you (pl.); *sārdhaṁ* - with; *baddhvā* - having bound; *nibhṛta* - solitary; *tamasi* - in the darkness; *kṣepsyati* - will throw; *drāk* - at once; *guhā* - a cave; *antaḥ* - within.

"O intelligent Lalite! You're trying to pay Me only half of My levy by hiding these best items (the intimate parts) from Me with different tricks and pleas. Can it ever be? See, My clerk Madhumangala, the king's spy, and Ujjvala, the king's dear, most intelligent

inspector is here. They are always trying to find faults in Me. If they secretly tell him this, that hardhearted king Cupid is quickly going to throw Me in a dark mountain cave, binding Me up with you *gopīs*!" (138-139)

Notes: Ujjvala is mentioned as follows in Śrīla Rūpa Gosvāmī's 'Rādhā-Kṛṣṇa Gaṇoddeśa Dīpikā' — *mūrtimān eva rasa-rāḍ ujjvalaś ca mahojjvalaḥ; vilāsi śekharo yasya vilāsena vaśīkṛtaḥ* — "Ujjvala is the most brilliant, and he is the embodiment of the emperor of *rasas* (eros). Vilāsi Śekhara (the most playful Śrī Kṛṣṇa) is subdued by his pastimes." *atra nikuñja kandarāyāṁ milanam eva saṁsūcyate* — The last line of these verses indicate a meeting in a *nikuñja*.

iti nāndīmukhī sākṣāc chāṁsite kaṁsa-vidviṣā
kapaṭa krodha vidhāddhā rādhā mādhavam abravīt

sad dharmodyat kamala-paṭala prauḍha rājīva-bandhor
gopendrasya prathita tanayaḥ śuddha rāmānujo'pi
duṣṭa dhvaṁsī svayam api vadasy āśu durbhāṣitaṁ yat
tat te sevākula phalam idaṁ divya ghaṭṭīṣu devyāḥ

iti - thus; *nāndīmukhī* - Nāndīmukhī; *sākṣāt* - personally; *śāṁsite* - spoken; *kaṁsa-vidviṣā* - by Kaṁsa's enemy (Kṛṣṇa); *kapaṭa* - false; *krodha* - anger; *viddhā* - pierced; *addhā* - easily; *rādhā* - Rādhā; *mādhavam* - to Mādhava; *abravīt* - spoke. *sat* - true; *dharma* - virtue; *udyat* - arising; *kamala-paṭala* -lotusflowers; *prauḍha* - blossomed; *rājīva* - lotus; *bandhoḥ* - of the friend (the sun); *gopendrasya* - of the king of the cowherds; *prathita* - well-known; *tanayaḥ* - son; *śuddha* - pure; *rāma* - Balarāma; *anujaḥ* - the younger brother; *api* - even; *duṣṭa* - of the wicked; *dhvaṁsī* - destroyer; *svayam* - personally; *api* - even; *vadasi* - you speak; *āśu* - swiftly; *durbhāṣitaṁ* -

crooked words; *yat* - what; *tat* -that; *te* - Your; *sevā* - service; *kula* - abundance; *phalam* - the fruit; *idaṁ* - this; *divya* - divine; *ghaṭṭīṣu* - of the toll-stations; *devyāḥ* - of the goddess.

When Kṛṣṇa personally told this to Nāndīmukhī, Rādhā, whose mind was pierced by false anger, told Mādhava: "Although You are the celebrated son of Nanda, the king of cowherders, who is like the full sunshine on the lotusflower of piety, the younger brother of pure-hearted Balarāma and the destroyer of the wicked, You are speaking such bad words now. This can only be the result of Your service to the goddess of this beautiful tollstation!" (140-141)

> *anyad atra ca yat kiñcin na brūte lajjayā sakhī*
> *tac chṛnu tvam iti vyājāt tuṅgavidyā jagāda tam*

> *ātma gahvaram abhaṅga bhujaṅga*
> *tvaṁ vraja drutam ito'ti cañcala*
> *āhi-tuṇḍika varā'bhimanyukaḥ*
> *sārthakāhvaya upaiti na yāvat*

anyat - another; *atra* - here; *ca* - and; *yat* - what; *kiñcit* - something; *na* - not; *brūte* - saying; *lajjayā* - with shame; *sakhī* - girlfriend; *tat* - that; *śṛnu* - listen; *tvam* - you; *iti* - thus; *vyājāt* - deceiving; *tuṅgavidyā* - Tuṅgavidyā; *jagāda* - said; *tam* - to Him. *ātma* - self; *gahvaram* - hole; *abhaṅga* - untameable, *nirantara kāma-krīḍā-śīla, adamya rati pipāsu iti vā, pakṣe — durdānta sarpaḥ* someone who always engages in erotic play, or whose erotic thirst cannot be quenched; *bhujaṅga* - snake; *tvaṁ* - you; *vraja* - go; *drutam* - swiftly; *itaḥ* - from here; *ati* - very; *cañcala* - restless; *āhi* - snake; *tuṇḍika* - catcher; *vara* - the best; *abhimanyukaḥ* - anger, or Rādhā's would-be husband; *sārthaka* -

appropriate; *āhvaya* - named; *upa* - close; *eti* - comes; *na* - not; *yāvat* - until.

Then Tuṅgavidyā slyly told Kṛṣṇa: "Listen to what my *sakhī* Rādhā could not tell You out of shyness: 'O Abhaṅga bhujaṅga (one who always engages in love-play, or whose thirst for erotic play cannot be quenched, or an untameable snake)! As long as Abhimanyu (a snake-catcher, or Rādhā's husband, who lives up to his name) does not come, You'd better quickly leave for Your own cave (home)" (142-143)

Notes: *yathā āhi-tuṇḍikasyāgre sarpasya cāñcalyaṁ na jāyate, tathā rādhā-pater abhimanyoḥ sakāśe ati kāmukasya tasya rasa cāñcalyam api dūrīgacched iti bāhyārthaḥ* "Just as the snake will not be naughty in front of the snake-charmer, similarly the *rasika* naughtiness of the lusty boy will disappear when Rādhā's husband Abhimanyu is around." This is the external meaning. *svābhiyoga-pakṣe tu ātma-gahvaraṁ girirāja-gahvaraṁ gaccha — yāvat na ko'pi āgacchatīti bhāvaḥ* The inner meaning is — "Quickly go to Your own cave in Girirāja Govardhana as long as nobody comes."

yeṣāṁ bhrāmyati padminī
phala-yugaṁ raktaṁ catuṣpaṅkajīm
bandhūke bhramarau vidhūṁś ca
dadhatī sārddha trayoviṁśatim
śyāmendo parapuṁsa āvakalanāt phullābhavet sā sadā
svīya svāmi raver vilokana bharan mlānā sphuṭaṁ tāmyati

yeṣāṁ - of those; *bhrāmyati* - wandering around; *padminī* - lotus-vine, or the best of women; *phala-yugaṁ* - a pair of fruits, or a pair of breasts; *raktaṁ* - red; *catuṣpaṅkajīm* - four lotuses, viz. the hands and feet;

bandhūke - the upper and lower lips; *bhramarau* - two bees, or pupils; *vidhūm* - moons; *ca* - and; *dadhatī* - manifest; *sārddha* - with one half; *trayoviṁśatim* - twenty-three - *vidhun - mukhe ekaḥ gaṇḍa-dvaye dvau, lalāṭe arddhaḥ tathā kara-pāda-nakhareṣu viṁśatir iti)* one being the face, two the cheeks, half the forehead and the other twenty the fingernails and toenails; *śyāmendoḥ* - of the blue moon, or our Śyāmasundara; *parapuṁsa* - paramour, or the best of men; *āvakalanāt* - at first sight; *phullābhavet* - blossomed; *sā* - she; *sadā* - always; *svīya* - own; *svāmi* - master; *raveḥ* - of the sun; *vilokana bharat* - from the sight; *mlānā* - fading; *sphuṭaṁ* - manifest; *tāmyati* - becomes colourless, turning pale, waning.

"A female lotus that has two fruits (breasts), four red lotusflowers (hands and feet), two Bandulī-flowers (lips) and two bees (pupils) as well as 23-and a half moons (face, cheeks, half for the forehead and twenty nails) wanders around, always blossoms when the blue moon (Śyāma-cānd) of Her paramour shines, but whithers away and dries up when She sees Her husband, the (Abhimanyu) sun!" (144)

Notes: *atrāti-śayoktyā padminyāḥ asambhava-sambhava-kārite mahādbhutatvaṁ vyajya sva pati ravi-kiraṇa-samparkam asahyaṁ manyamānāyās tasyāḥ para puruṣa-candra-kiraṇa-sahavāsena praphullatvaṁ vijñāpya virodhābhāsena parama rasa camatkāritvaṁ pradarśitam* "Here, with the metaphor of *atiśayokti*, the lotus flower is seen to make the impossible possible and this is causing great wonder. She cannot tolerate the sunrays provided by Her husband, but blossoms when She lives in the company of Her paramour, who showers Her with moonbeams instead. This is wholly contrary to the natural behaviour of lotus flowers and therefore this shows great *rasika* astonishment.

iti hari mukha-padma kṣveli saurabhya-sadma
prati-vacana madhūni prīnitaitat sabhāni
tad ati racita bādhāpīyam āpīya rādhā
prakaṭa rucam udārāṁ vācam ārād uvāca
kumāra bhaja dhīratāṁ na kuru durmadāc cāpalaṁ
purī nikaṭa vartinī duradhipo'tra kaṁso valī
atas tava hitaṁ bruve vrajamahendra sambandhataḥ
samūhya gahanaṁ vraja prakaṭam atra gāś cāraya

iti - thus; *hari* - Hari; *mukha* - face; *padma* - lotus; *kṣveli* - humour; *saurabhya* - of sweet fragrance; *sadma* - abode; *prati-vacana* - answer; *madhūni* - the honey; *prīnita* - pleased; *etat* - that; *sabhāni* - in the assembly; *tat* - that; *ati* - very much; *racita* - made; *bādhā* - obstacle; *api* - even; *iyam* - this; *āpīya* - drinking; *rādhā* - Rādhā; *prakaṭa* - manifest; *rucam* - desire; *udārāṁ* - honest; *vācam* - words; *ārāt* - from afar; *uvāca* - spoke. *kumāra* - celibate boy; *bhaja* - worship; *dhīratāṁ* - patience; *na* - not; *kuru* - do; *durmadāt* - out of infatuation; *cāpalaṁ* - restless; *purī* - Mathurā; *nikaṭa* - close by; *vartinī* - staying; *duḥ* - bad; *adhipaḥ* - king; *atra* - here; *kaṁsaḥ* - Kaṁsa; *balī* - powerful; *ataḥ* - then; *tava* - your; *hitaṁ* - benefit; *bruve* - I speak; *vraja* - of Vraja; *mahā* - great; *indra* - king; *sambandhataḥ* - from the relationship; *samūhya* - understanding My words; *gahanaṁ* - to the forest; *vraja* - go; *prakaṭam* - clearly; *atra* - here; *gāḥ* - cows; *cāraya* - herd.

The relishable honey-like joking answer that streamed from Hari's lotuslike mouth gladdened all the assembled *gopīs*. Śrī Rādhā fully drank that honey, although it caused a great obstacle to Her going to the sacrifice. From afar She spoke the following gentle words: "O young boy! Be patient! Don't be naughty! Mathurā-purī is close by and the wicked king Kaṁsa is very powerful! I speak for Your sake, because You're the

son of the king of Vraja: go back to the forest and show that You are tending Your cows there!" (145-146)

Notes: *atrāpi svābhiyogaḥ — kumāraḥ kutsito māraḥ kandarpaḥ rasa-cāñcalya vistārasya sthānāsthāna-vicārābhāvāt — atc gahanam araṇyam vraja, tatraiva tava rasa-cāñcalyaṁ yukti-yuktaṁ, tathā indriyāṇām api sucāru tarpaṇādikaṁ tatraiva bhāvīti dyotatam* — Here the pun is: *kumāra* means ugly Cupid, who extends his naughtiness without considering the place. Therefore go to the deep forest, that is the proper place for naughty activities. There the senses will be nicely gratified...

> *mahā madana bhū-pater ayam abhinna dehaḥ svarāt*
> *nṛśaṁsa nṛpa jīvitā'dhika vayasya keśyādikān*
> *vimathya dara līlayā sphurati yo'tra goṣṭhāntare*
> *sa eṣa tava kaṁsataḥ sakhi vibheti kiṁ me sakhā*

> *athaiṣa pṛthu manmatho ya iha tasya sāmāntakaḥ*
> *sa eva laghu manmathaḥ param amuṣya kaṁso vaśaḥ*
> *ato'sya lipim aṅkitaṁ sapadi tatra nītvā dadan*
> *nṛpāt kaṭakam ānayan patikulāni badhnāmi vaḥ*

mahā - the great; *madana* - Cupid; *bhūpateḥ* - of the king; *ayam* - this; *abhinna* - non-different; *dehaḥ* - body; *svarāt* - emperor; *nṛśaṁsa* - cruel; *nṛpa* - king; *jīvitā* - than life; *adhika* - more; *vayasya* -friends; *keśī* - Keśī; *ādikān* - beginning with; *vimathya* - killing; *dara* - slight; *līlayā* - playful; *sphurati* - is manifest; *yaḥ* - who; *atra* - here; *goṣṭha* - Vraja; *antare* - inside; *sa eṣa* - He; *tava* - your; *kaṁsataḥ* - from Kaṁsa; *sakhi* - friend; *vibheti* - fears; *kiṁ* - what; *me* - my; *sakhā* - friend. *atha* - then; *eṣa* - this; *pṛthu* - great; *manmathaḥ* - Cupid; *ya* - who; *iha* - here; *tasya* - his; *sāmāntakaḥ* - subordinate king; *sa* - he; *eva* - surely; *laghu* - small; *manmathaḥ* - Cupid (*catur-vyūhāntargata pradyumnyākhyaḥ śākhā-sthānīyaḥ kāma ityaỉthaḥ śrī krṣṇa-karṇāmṛtoktvāt* — It is described in Kṛṣṇa Karṇāmṛta that Kāmadeva is situated in the Pradyumna-branch of Śrī Viṣṇu's *catur-vyūha*); *param* - greatest; *amuṣya* - his; *kaṁsaḥ* - Kaṁsa; *vaśaḥ* - control; *ataḥ* - thus; *asya* - His; *lipim* - letter; *aṅkitaṁ* - hand-signed; *sapadi* - suddenly; *tatra* -there; *nītvā* - having taken; *dadan* - giving; *nṛpāt* - from the king; *kaṭakam* - army; *ānayan* - bringing; *pati* - husband; *kulāni* - of the family; *badhnāmi* - I shall bind; *vaḥ* - you.

Madhumaṅgala said: "O Sakhi! Kṛṣṇa is non-different from king Cupid. He is a great emperor who callously killed demons like Keśī here in Vraja, who were friends of the cruel king Kaṁsa, that were dearer to him than life! Should He be afraid of Kaṁsa? You see, my friend Kṛṣṇa is the great transcendental king Cupid, and the small (material) king Cupid is just His lieutenant, who easily subdues this king Kaṁsa. So I'm quickly going to king Kaṁsa with a signed letter from my friend (Kṛṣṇa) to ask him to bring an army here to bind up your husbands!" (147-148)

itīha madhumaṅgalollasita vaktra kañja skhalad
vacaḥ prasara sauṣṭhavocchalita sīdhu-dhārām imam
nipīya rabhasonmada mṛduṁ dadhāra hāsa dhvaniṁ
sadaḥ sarasi sundarī rasika sabhya bhṛṅgyāvalī

iti - thus; *iha* - here; *madhumaṅgala* - Madhumaṅgala; *ullasita* - jubilant; *vaktra* - face; *kañja* - lotus; *skhalad* - emanating; *vacaḥ* - words; *prasara* - multitude; *sauṣṭhava* - elegant; *ucchalita* - arising; *sīdhu* - nectar; *dhārām* - stream; *imam* - this; *nipīya* - drinking; *rabhasa* - with great ecstasy; *unmada* - inebriated; *mṛduṁ* - soft; *dadhāra* - manifest; *hāsa* - laughing; *dhvaniṁ* - sound;

sadaḥ - assembly; *sarasi* - the lake; *sundarī* - beautiful; *rasika* - *rasika;* *sabhya* - in the assembly; *bhṛṅgī* - she-bees; *āvalī* - the multitude.

Hearing these honey-like words flowing from Madhumaṅgala's lotuslike mouth in such an exquisite way, the beautiful bee-like *rasika gopīs* from the lake-like *gopī*-assembly became intoxicated with ecstasy and laughed softly and sweetly. (149)

etat tad uktam adhigatya mṛṣā ruṣā'yam
vācaṁ rucā'ti-rucirām iti tām uvāca
dānaṁ na ced dadati me tad imā mayaiva
sārdhaṁ calantviha mahā madanendra pārśvam

etat - that; *tat* - this; *uktam* - said; *adhigatya* - having understood; *mṛṣā* - false; *ruṣā* - with anger; *ayam* - He; *vācam* - words; *rucā* - with desire; *ati* - very; *rucirām* - beautiful; *iti* - thus; *tām* - She; *uvāca* - spoke; *dānam* - taxation; *na* - not; *cet* - if; *dadati* - gives; *me* - to Me; *tat* - that; *imāḥ* - these girls; *mayā* - by Me; *eva* - certainly; *sārdham* - along with; *calantu* - may move; *iha* - here; *mahā* - great; *madana* - Cupid; *indra* - king; *pārśvam* - on the side.

Understanding Madhumaṅgala's jokes, Kṛṣṇa told the most lustrous Rādhā with false anger: "If You don't pay Your tax you must all come with Me to the great king Cupid!" (150)

ko vā mahā manasijaḥ sakhi naiva jāne
kutrāpi na śrutacaro jagatītale'sau
mithyaiṣa yan mahima nāma balāni tasya
saṅkīrtayet tad iha vaḥ parihāsa bhaṅgyaiḥ

kaḥ - who; *vā* - or; *mahā* - great; *manasijaḥ* - Cupid; *sakhi* - O girlfriend!; *na* - not; *eva* - certainly; *jāne* - know;

kutrāpi - anywhere; *na* - not; *śruta-caraḥ* - heard; *jagatī-tale* - on the surface of the earth; *asau* - that; *mithyā* - false; *eṣa* - this; *yat* - that; *mahima* - glories; *nāma* - name; *balāni* - and power; *tasya* - his; *saṅkīrtayet* - must glorify; *tat* - that; *iha* - here; *vaḥ* - your; *parihāsa* - joking; *bhaṅgyaiḥ* - through gestures.

"O *Sakhi*!", Campakalatā said, "I don't know who that great king Cupid is, nor has anyone else in the world ever heard of him! Your glorification of his name, glory and prowess was all false, and Your jokes were also just for fun!" (151)

ityādya campakalatā lapitaṁ tadānīm
ākarṇya gokula-vidhur vidhu-vaktra bimbām
rādhāṁ nirīkṣya dara bhāṣitavān sabhāyāṁ
sollunṭham indu-vadane madano'dvitīyaḥ

atraiva hṛdya girivarya visṛṣṭa paṭṭa
rāṣṭre virājati mahā madanaḥ sadaiva
tat sevikābhir api yad bhavatībhir evam
ābhāṣyate tad iha vo mada eva hetuḥ

iti - thus; *ādya* - beginning with; *campakalatā* - Campakalatā; *lapitaṁ* - spoken; *tadānīm* - then; *ākarṇya* - having heard; *gokula-vidhuḥ* - the moon of Gokula; *vidhu-vaktra* - moon-face; *bimbām* - the globe; *rādhām* - Rādhā; *nirīkṣya* - seeing; *dara* - slightly; *bhāṣitavān* - speaker; *sabhāyāṁ* - in the assembly; *sa* - with; *ullunṭham* - sarcasm; *indu-vadane* - O moon-faced girl!; *madanaḥ* - Cupid; *advitīyaḥ* - unrivalled. *atra* - here; *eva* - certainly; *hṛdya* - pleasant; *giri* - mountain; *varya* - best; *visṛṣṭa* - created; *paṭṭa rāṣṭre* - in the kingdom; *virājati* - remains; *mahā* - great; *madanaḥ* - Cupid; *sadā* - always; *eva* - certainly; *tat* - that; *sevikābhiḥ* - with maidservants; *api* - even; *yat* -

which; *bhavatībhiḥ* - by you (pl., fem.); *evam* - thus; *ābhāṣyate* - spoke; *tat* - that; *iha* - here; *vaḥ* - your; *mada* - pride; *eva* - certainly; *hetuḥ* - the cause.

"O Moon-faced girl! Hearing these sweet words of Campakalatā, Śrī Kṛṣṇa, the moon of Gokula, who is nondifferent from Cupid, looked at moonfaced Rādhikā just once and then sarcastically told the *gopīs:* **"Here, by this best of charming mountains, the unrivalled Cupid always resides. It's only out of pride that you are speaking in this way, although you're all his maidservants!"** (152-153)

saṁlabhya satra sadane gamane'dya bādhāṁ
rādhā mudhā sphurita roṣa rasābhiṣiktā
tiryak sphuran nayana nartana tīvra bāṇair
āvidhya kṛṣṇam adhunā madhuvāg uvāca

he vīra ballaba-vadhū vadanāravinda
mādhvīka pāna-bharataḥ paramāti śuddha
bhāgyāt tvayā saha yayā calitaṁ varākṣyā
bāḍhaṁ rarakṣa gṛha-dharma kulāni saiva

saṁlabhya - attaining; *satra* - sacrifice; *sadane* - in the abode; *gamane* - in the going; *adya* -now; *bādhām* - obstruction; *rādhā* - Rādhā; *mudhā* - vainly, or falsely; *sphurita* - manifested; *roṣa* - anger; *rasa* - with nectar; *abhiṣiktā* - sprinkled; *tiryak* - crooked; *sphurat* - manifested; *nayana* - eyes; *nartana* - dancing; *tīvra* - sharp; *bāṇaiḥ* - with arrows; *āvidhya* - pierced; *kṛṣṇam* - Kṛṣṇa; *adhunā* - now; *madhu* - honey; *vāk* - words; *uvāca* - spoke. *he* - O!; *vīra* - hero; *ballaba-vadhū* - cowherd-wife; *vadana* - face; *aravinda* - lotus; *mādhvīka* - honey; *pāna* - drinking; *bharataḥ* - greatly; *parama* - supreme; *ati* - very; *śuddha* - pure; *bhāgyāt* - by good fortune; *tvayā saha* - with you;

yayā - by whom (fem.); *calitaṁ* - moved; *varākṣyā* - by the fair-eyed girls; *bāḍhaṁ* - greatly; *rarakṣa* - protecting; *gṛha-* household; *dharma* - duties; *kulāni* - multitude; *sā* - She; *eva* - certainly.

Being obstructed in Her going to the sacrifice, Rādhikā was showered by false anger and spoke the following sweet words to Kṛṣṇa, piercing Him with the sharp arrows of Her crooked dancing eyes: "O Hero! You are most purified by drinking the honey of the *gopīs'* lotus-like faces! It is fortunate that this fair-eyed lady, that is sufficiently protecting religious family principles, has come with You!" (154-155)

Notes: *atra viparīta-lakṣaṇayā solluṇṭha-vacanam idaṁ tena ca tasyāḥ iha para-kāla dharma-jātāni sarvāṇyevāstamitānīti mahā-durbhāgyaṁ tasyāḥ sūcitam* — These are sarcastic words with a contrary purpurt. By Him Her pious merit both in this life and the next is destroyed. Thus Her great misfortune is indicated.

dṛṣṭvā tayoḥ kalim analpa rasātibaddham
ācāryayor vividha narma-kalā kalāpe
śāntīcchayā vinaya vākya-kulais tato'sau
nāndīmukhī samabhinandya hariṁ jagāda

dānīndra māṅgalika yajña nimittam etāḥ
śuddhā nayanti śirasā nava gavya-kumbhān
dharmaṁ nirīkṣya kula-candra vimuñca tasmāt
kāmaṁ yathā bhavati te yaśasi pracāraḥ

dṛṣṭvā - having seen; *tayoḥ* - of both; *kalim* - quarrel; *analpa* - great; *rasa* - flavour; *ati* - greatly; *baddham* - bound; *ācāryayoḥ* - of the two teachers; *vividha* - different kinds; *narma* - humour; *kalā* - arts; *kalāpe* - of the multitude; *śānti* - peace; *icchayā* - by the desire; *vinaya* - humble; *vākya* - words; *kulaiḥ* - with the hosts; *tataḥ* - then; *asau* - she; *nāndīmukhī* - Nāndīmukhī; *samabhinandya* - congratulating; *harim* - to Hari; *jagāda* - said. *dānī* - tax-collector; *indra* - king; *māṅgalika* - auspicious; *yajña* - sacrifice; *nimittam* - the cause; *etāḥ* - they; *śuddhā* - pure; *nayanti* - bring; *śirasā* - with the head; *nava* - fresh; *gavya* - dairy products; *kumbhān* - jugs; *dharmam* - virtue; *nirīkṣya* - seeing; *kula* - of the family; *candra* - moon; *vimuñca* - leave in peace; *tasmāt* - from that; *kāmam* - enhance; *yathā* - just as; *bhavati* - is; *te* - your; *yaśasi* - in fame; *pracāraḥ* - proclamation.

Seeing this very humorous quarrel of the Rasika Yugala, that are the teachers of different humorous arts, Nāndīmukhī became eager to make peace, so humbly and respectfully she told Śrī Hari: "O King of toll-collectors! These *gopīs* have come to this auspicious sacrifice with a pure mind, carrying pots with fresh *ghī* on their heads! Therefore, O moon of Your family, cast a glance at virtue and leave them alone! This will enhance Your reputation!" (156-157)

girīndra purataḥ sphuran nava sarovarasyonnata
prasannatara vāriṇaḥ kusuma-saṅgha sad gandhinaḥ
dhvanāḍhya khaga saṅginaḥ parita eva sa bhūruhaiḥ
samṛddham adhikam vanam jayati yatra khelāspade

kvacit kvacana sundaram raṇati matta bhṛṅgāvalī
madhu prasara mandire surabhi puṣpa-vṛndodare
kvacit kvacana kokilāḥ kala rutāni saṁtanvate
rasāla vana mañjarī vara maranda pānonmadaḥ
kvacit kvacana kekinaḥ pṛthu naṭanti kecin madāt
kvacit kvacana kecana pratinadanti cāmodinaḥ
kvacit kvacana mādhurī bhara rasāla hṛdyojjvalat
phala prakara bhakṣaṇe paṭu raṭanti śārī śukāḥ

śvas tāvad etat saraso nikuñjam
etāḥ sameṣyanti mahān api tvam
tatraiva yuktaṁ tava dānam etat
sampādayiṣyāmy atha lagnikāham
yato'tra nirvartyam idaṁ hi dānaṁ
girau sthitasyāsya sarovarasya
tad dāna nivartanam ity abhikhyā
bhaviṣyatīty eva hi sā jagāda

giri - mountain; *indra* - mountain; *purataḥ* - before; *sphurat* - manifesting; *nava* -fresh; *sarovarasya* - of the lake; *unnata* - raised; *prasannatara* - clear; *vāriṇaḥ* - with water; *kusuma-saṅgha* -by a host of flowers; *sat* - true; *gandhinaḥ* - with scents; *dhvana* - sounds; *aḍhya* - enriched; *khaga* - bird; *saṅginaḥ* - with the contact; *parita* - all around; *eva* - certainly; *sa* - he; *bhū-ruhaiḥ* - by the trees; *samṛddham* - beautiful; *adhikaṁ* - greater; *vanaṁ* - forest; *jayati* - glorious; *yatra* - where; *khelāspade* -playground. *kvacit* - sometimes; *kvacana* - somewhere; *sundaraṁ* - beautiful; *raṇati* - humming; *matta* - drunken; *bhṛṅga* - bee; *āvalī* - swarm; *madhu* - honey; *prasara* - flowing; *mandire* - in the grove; *surabhi* - fragrant; *puṣpa* - flowers; *vṛnda* - host; *udare* - in the womb; *kvacit* - sometimes; *kvacana* - somewhere; *kokilāḥ* - cuckoos; *kala* - unclear; *rutāni* - sweet sounds; *saṁtanvate* - expanding; *rasāla* -mango; *vana* - forest; *mañjarī* - buds; *vara* - best; *maranda* - honey; *pāna* - drinking; *unmadaḥ* - intoxicated. *kvacit* - sometimes; *kvacana* - somewhere; *kekinaḥ* - peacocks; *pṛthu* - brashly; *naṭanti* - they dance; *kecit* - some; *madāt* - out of joy; *kvacit* - sometimes; *kvacana* - somewhere; *kecana* - some; *prati-nadanti* - echoing; *ca* - and; *amodinaḥ* - blissfully; *kvacit* - sometimes; *kvacana* - somewhere; *mādhurī* - sweetness; *bhara* - greatly; *rasāla* - mango; *hṛdya* - pleasant; *ujjvalat* - glistening; *phala* -fruits; *prakara* - multitude; *bhakṣaṇe* - in eating; *paṭuḥ* - greatly; *raṭanti* - resounding; *sārī* - female parrot; *śukāḥ* - male parrot. *śvaḥ* - tomorrow; *tāvat* - until then; *etat* - this; *sarasaḥ* - lake; *nikuñjam* - grove; *etāḥ* - they; *sameṣyanti* - they will come; *mahān* - great; *api* - even; *tvam* - you; *tatra* - there; *eva* - certainly; *yuktaṁ* - proper; *tava* - Your; *dānam* - toll-payment; *etat* - this; *sampādayiṣyāmy* - I will accomplish; *atha* - then; *lagnikā* - guarantee; *aham* - I. *yataḥ* - because; *atra* - here; *nirvartyam* - accomplished; *idaṁ* - this; *hi* - certainly; *dānaṁ* - toll; *girau* - on Govardhana Hill; *sthitasya* - situated; *asya* - of that; *sarovarasya* - of the lake; *tat* - that; *dāna nivartanam* - Dāna Nirvartana; *iti* - thus; *abhikhyā* - named; *bhaviṣyati* - it will be; *iti* - thus; *eva* - certainly; *hi* - indeed; *sā* - she; *jagāda* - said.

atroddīpana vibhāvaḥ khalu varṇyate — This is certainly a description of *uddīpana vibhāva* various incitements for Kṛṣṇa-consciousness — "There is a very beautiful forest with beautiful trees around a new lake (Mānasa Gaṅgā) filled with fragrant flowers, singing birds and very clear water in front of Govardhana Hill. In the honey-showering *kuñja*-playgrounds around this lake intoxicated bees sometimes buzz beautifully around the whorls of the fragrant lotusflowers, the cuckoos sometimes sing sweetly and indistinctly, being intoxicated by the honey of the best buds of the mango forest, filling all directions with their chirping. Elsewhere intoxicated peacocks sometimes frantically dance, somewhere other peacocks sometimes blissfully echo the mewing of these peacocks, and again elsewhere the male and female parrots sometimes sing, eating sweet, juicy glistening fruits. Tomorrow They are coming here to the bank of this (Mānasa Gaṅgā) lake, o sir, you also come please! I guarantee you the proper payment of Your tax! On the bank of this lake near Govardhana Hill the tax will be returned, so this place will be named Dāna

Nirvartana kuṇḍa." After saying this, Sumukhī fell silent. (158-162)

anena tasyā vacanena tena
vihasya muktāḥ smita cāru vaktrāḥ
taṁ vīkṣamānā nayanāñcalais tāś
celur mudā yajña gṛhāya pūrṇāḥ

anena - by this; *tasyā* - her; *vacanena* - with the word; *tena* - by Kṛṣṇa; *vihasya* - laughing; *muktāḥ* - freed; *smita* - smile; *cāru* - beautiful; *vaktrāḥ* - face; *taṁ* - him; *vīkṣamānā* - being seen; *nayana* - eyes; *añcalaiḥ* - with the corners; *tāḥ* - they; *celuḥ* - went; *mudā* - joyfully; *yajña* - sacrifice; *gṛhāya* - to the abode; *pūrṇāḥ* - fulfilled desires.

Smilingly Kṛṣṇa fulfilled their desires there, and then released them, and the *gopīs* with their beautiful sweet slightly smiling faces looked at Him here from the corners of their eyes, blissfully proceeding to the sacrificial arena. (163)

Notes: *atra 'pūrṇāḥ' ityanena pūrṇa manorathā ityarthe āyāte śrī dāna keli kaumudyukta diśā śrī rādhā-mādhavayos tatraiva rahaḥ keli kuñje lalitādibhiḥ praveśaḥ kāritaḥ — nibhṛta vilāsa samāpanānte ca bahir āgatau yugala kiśorau — tad anantaraṁ ca tā muktā iti jñeyaṁ sarvaṁ samañjasaṁ ceti dik. uktaṁ ca — śrī dāsa gosvāmibhir dāna nirvartana kuṇḍāṣṭake - nija nija nava kuñje guñji rolamba puñje praṇayi nava sakhībhiḥ sampraveśya priyau tau ityādinā.* The word *pūrṇā* means that their desires were fulfilled. Śrī Dāna Keli Kaumudī states that Śrī Rādhā and Mādhava entered a solitary grove there with Lalitā and the *sakhīs*. After completing the intimate enjoyment the Yugala Kiśora came out again. After that they were all released. It is also said in Śrī Dāsa

Gosvāmī's 'Dāna Nirvartana Kuṇḍāṣṭaka' - "May we reside at Dāna Nirvartana kuṇḍa, where the young loving *sakhīs* make the Youthful Loving Couple enter into their own fresh *kuñjas* that are filled with buzzing bees, and where they make Them enjoy incomparible, ever-fresh pastimes!"

> *kṛṣṇākṣi matta madhupe nija dṛṣṭi-bhṛṅgīṁ*
> *bhaṅgyā parisphurad ananga taraṅgitāṅgī*
> *grīvārdha bhaṅga ruciraṁ dara yojayantī*
> *smitvālivarga valitā calitātha rādhā*

krṣna - Kṛṣṇa; *akṣi* - eyes; *matta* - intoxicated; *madhupe* - in the honeybee; *nija* - own; *dṛṣṭi*- eyes; *bhṛṅgīṁ* - she-bee; *bhaṅgyā* - with a gesture; *parisphurad* - manifesting; *ananga* - Cupid; *taraṅgita* - tossed about by the waves; *aṅgī* - her limbs; *grīva* - the neck; *ardha* - half; *bhaṅga* - crooked; *ruciraṁ* - charming; *dara* - slightly; *yojayantī* - engaging; *smitvā* - having smiled; *ali*- girlfriends; *varga* - group; *valitā* - surrounded; *calita* - went; *atha* - then; *rādhā* - Rādhā.

With some gestures Śrī Rādhikā fixed Her bee-like eyes at Kṛṣṇa's drunken bee-like eyes, and waves of desire appeared on all of Her limbs. She slightly bent Her neck and after standing there for some time in a very charming way, She smiled and went along, surrounded by Her girlfriends. (164)

> *tadaiva tāsāṁ mukha-paṅkajānāṁ*
> *smita sphuran mañju maranda bindum*
> *netrānta vaktrena piban nitāntaṁ*
> *mukunda bhṛṅgo mudam āpa so'pi*

tadā - then; *eva* - certainly; *tāsāṁ* - their (fem.) *mukha* - face; *paṅkajānāṁ* - of the lotusflowers; *smita* -

smile; *sphurat* - manifesting; *mañju* - lovely; *maranda* - honey; *bindum* - drops; *netra* - eyes; *anta* - corners; *vaktrena* - with the mouth; *piban* - drinking; *nitāntam* - greatly; *mukunda* - Mukunda; *bhṛṅgaḥ* - bee; *mudam* - joyfully; *āpa* - attainedl; *saḥ* - he; *api* - even.

The bee-like Mukunda also became very happy, always drinking the honeydrops of the *gopīs'* **softly smiling lotuslike faces through the mouth of the corners of His eyes. (165)**

> *tato vayasyaiḥ saha nāgaro'sau*
> *govardhanādreḥ śiraso'vataṁsaḥ*
> *gāś cārayan dāna kathāmṛtaṁ tat*
> *kurvan mitho modam avāpa kṛṣṇaḥ*

tataḥ - then; *vayasyaiḥ saha* - with His friends; *nāgaraḥ* - hero Kṛṣṇa; *asau* - this; *govardhana* - Govardhana; *adreḥ* - of the mountain; *śirasaḥ* - on the head; *avataṁsaḥ* - the ornament; *gāḥ* - cows; *cārayan* - herding; *dāna kathā* - topics of the tax-pastime; *amṛtaṁ* - nectar; *tat* - that; *kurvan* - doing; *mithaḥ* - mutual; *modam* - delight; *avāpa* - attained; *kṛṣṇaḥ* - Kṛṣṇa.

Then Nāgara Śrī Kṛṣṇa and His friends tended their cows on top of Govardhana Hill, looking like the ornament of the Hill, and blissfully discussed the nectarean story of the Dāna-*līlā* with Each other. (166)

> *kāntyā diśo daśa muhur guru gaurayantī*
> *bhrājad dṛganta naṭanair ati nīlayantī*
> *sāpi smitārdha kalayā pariśuklayantī*
> *vārtāmṛtair madhurayanty uru satram āpa*

kāntyā - with her luster; *diśaḥ* - directions; *daśa* - ten; *muhuḥ* - repeatedly; *guru* - great; *gaurayantī* - making golden; *bhrājad* - illuminating; *dṛganta* - side long glances; *naṭanaiḥ* - with the dancing; *ati* - greatly; *nīlayantī* - turning blue; *sā* - she; *api* - even; *smita* - smile; *ardha* - half; *kalayā* -with the fragment; *pariśuklayantī* - turning white; *vārtā* - topic; *amṛtaiḥ* - with the ambrosias; *madhurayanti* - turning sweet; *uru* - great; *satram* - sacrifice; *āpa* - attained.

Śrī Rādhikā constantly pervaded all directions with the golden effulgence of Her body, the blue effulgence of Her eyes and the white effulgence of Her sweet slight smile, sweetening all directions with the sound of Her descriptions of this story as She arrived at the place of the sacrifice. (167)

praṇamya gavyaṁ vinayena divyaṁ
pradāya tebhyo varabhūṣaṇādi
saṁlabhya ramyāṇi punaḥ svakuṇḍam
āsādya tās tat kathayā vijahruḥ

rejus tāḥ prema-saubhāgya saundaryādi guṇa śriyā
sārair munivarāl labdhair bhūṣaṇaiś ca vibhūṣitāḥ

praṇamya - offering obeisances; *gavyaṁ* - dairy products; *vinayena* - with humility; *divyaṁ* -divine; *pradāya* - giving; *tebhyaḥ* - to them; *vara* - great; *bhūṣaṇa* - ornaments; *ādi* - beginning; *saṁlabhya* - attaining; *ramyāṇi* - beautiful; *punaḥ* - again; *sva* - own; *kuṇḍam* - pond; *āsādya* - attaining; *tāḥ* - they (fem.) *tat* - that; *kathayā* - with the conversation; *vijahruḥ* - enjoyed. *rejuḥ* - appeared very splendid; *tāḥ* - they (fem.) *prema* - of love; *saubhāgya* - good fortune; *saundarya* - sweet; *ādi* - beginning; *guṇa* - attributes; *śriyā* - with the beauty; *sāraiḥ* - with the most excellent; *muni-varāt* - from the greatest sage; *labdhaiḥ* - with the attained (pl.); *bhūṣaṇaiḥ* - with the ornaments; *ca* - and; *vibhūṣitāḥ* - decorated.

The *gopīs* humbly offered their obeisances to the *munis*, gave them the *ghī*, collected the rewards of ornaments from them and then returned to the bank of Rādhākuṇḍa, blissfully discussing the topic of the Dāna līlā with each other and ornamenting themselves with the opulence of qualities like love, good fortune and beauty, as well as with the superb ornaments given to them by the best of sages (Bhāgurī) (168-169).

rādhā mahā prema rasābhiṣikta
smara kriyā śāstra viśāradā sā
suvihvalā sāttvika mukhya bhāvaiḥ
priyaṁ jagau prāṇa-sakhī vṛtoccaiḥ

rādhā - Rādhā; *mahā* - great; *prema* - love; *rasa* - flavour; *abhiṣikta* - sprinkling; *smara* - erotic; *kriyā* - activities; *śāstra* - scriptures; *viśāradā* - expert; *sā* - She; *su* - greatly; *vihvalā* - agitated; *sāttvika (kampāśru-svedādibhiḥ)* - *sāttvika bhāvas; mukhya* - main; *bhāvaiḥ* - with feelings; *priyaṁ* - beloved (m.); *jagau* - glorified; *prāṇa-sakhī* - heart's girlfriend; *vṛta* - surrounded; *uccaiḥ* - loudly.

Śrī Rādhikā, who is expert in the art of eros, was sprinkled by the nectar of great love, overwhelmed by the main *sāttvika* ecstasies (inertia, goosepimples, changing of voice and bodily colour, shedding tears, etc) as She loudly glorified the names of Her *priyatama* (beloved Kṛṣṇa) with Her girlfriends. (170)

trailokya-varti nava dampati mūrdhna-ratnaṁ
dagdha smarāṅga ghaṭanonnata siddha tantram
līlāvilāsa nava sarjana vedhasaṁ tad
yugmaṁ na varṇayitum abja-bhavo'pi śaktaḥ

trailokya - three worlds; *varti* - acting; *nava* - young; *dampati* - pair of lovers; *mūrdhna* - heart; *ratnaṁ* -

jewel; *dagdha* - burned; *smara* - Cupid; *aṅga* - body; *ghaṭana* - occurrence; *unnata* - exalted; *siddha* - perfect; *tantram* - formula; *līlā* - pastimes; *vilāsa* - pastimes; *nava* - new; *sarjana* - creation; *vedhasaṁ* - creator; *tat* - that; *yugmam* - couple; *na* - not; *varṇayitum* - describing; *abja-bhavaḥ* - Brahmā; *api* - even; *śaktaḥ* - is able.

Even Lord Brahmā is unable to describe that Yugala Kiśora that always creates new pastimes, that are the crownjewels of all young lovers of the three worlds, and who are expert in making perfect *tantras* for rejuvenating Cupid's body, that was previously burned by Śiva. (171)

iti vilasita vārtāṁ kundavallī rasāktāṁ
rahasi pariniśamy ānanda sindhau nimagnā
drutam atha nija sakhyā sā samṛddhā tayā'ddhā
tad iha mithuna ratnaṁ draṣṭum utkā cacāla

iti - thus; *vilasita* - of the pastimes; *vārtāṁ* - the narration; *kundavallī* - Kundalatā; *rasa* - flavours; *aktāṁ* - anointed; *rahasi* - in secret; *pariniśamya* - hearing; *ānanda* - bliss; *sindhau* - in the ocean; *nimagnā* - drowned; *drutam* - quickly; *atha* - then; *nija* - own; *sakhyā* - with her girl-friend Sumukhī; *sā* - She; *samṛddhā* - met; *tayā* - with her friend Sumukhī; *addhā* - personally; *tat* - that; *iha* -here; *mithuna* - pair of lovers; *ratnaṁ* - jewel; *draṣṭum* - to see; *utkā* - eager; *cacāla* - went.

Kundalatā drowned in an ocean of bliss when she privately heard this humorous story, and she eagerly went along with her dear friend Sumukhī to see that Yugala Kiśora. (172)

dadhy ādi dāna nava keli rasābdhi madhye
magnaṁ navīna yuva ratna yugaṁ vrajasya

narmāli hṛdyam udita dyuti gaura nīlam
andho'pi lubdha iva lokitum utsuko'smi

dadhi - yoghurt; *ādi* - beginning; *dāna* - taxation;
nava - new; *keli* - pastime; *rasa* - flavour; *abdhi* - ocean;
madhye - in the middle; *magnaṁ* - drowned; *navīna* - new;
yuva - youngsters; *ratna* -jewel; *yugaṁ* - pair; *vrajasya* - of
Vraja; *narma* - joking; *ali* - girlfriends; *hṛdyam* - pleasant;
udita - arising; *dyuti* - splendor; *gaura* - golden; *nīlam* -
blue; *andhaḥ* - blind; *api* - although; *lubdha* - greedy; *iva* -
as if; *lokitum* - to see; *utsukaḥ* - eager; *asmi* - I am.

**Although I am blind with ignorance I've become
eager like a greedy man to see the young, jewel-like
lovers of Vraja that are of golden and blue complexion,
that have many loving girlfriends and that are
immersed in a fresh *rasa*-ocean of pastimes around the
tax on things like yoghurt. (173)**

rādhā mādhavayor dāna keli cintāmaṇiṁ girau
labdham andhena vīkṣantāṁ śrīmad rūpa gaṇāḥ priyāḥ

rādhā mādhavayoḥ - of Rādhā and Mādhava; *dāna*
- taxation; *keli* - play; *cintāmaṇiṁ* - a gem; *girau* - at the
mountain; *labdham* - attained; *andhena* - by a blind man;
vīkṣantāṁ - seeing (relishing); *śrīmad rūpa* - Śrīla Rūpa
Gosvāmī; *gaṇāḥ* - the party; *priyāḥ* - beloved.

**This blind person has found the Cintāmaṇi-gem
of Rādhā and Mādhava's Dāna Keli at Govardhana Hill
and hopes that the followers of his beloved Śrīmad Rūpa
Gosvāmī will relish it. (174)**

Notes: *andhenetyanena svasya darśanāsāmarthaṁ*
dainyena   jñāpitam.   śrīmad   rūpa   gosvāmi-
caraṇāravindānugata rasika janā evāsya grantha-ratnasya

tātparyāvadhāraṇāyālam ityapi dyotitam anenādhikārī nirṇayo'pi kṛtaḥ "By using the word *andhena* (by a blind person) the author has humbly announced his own lack of qualification. The *rasika* followers of Śrīmad Rūpa Gosvāmī's lotusfeet are able to understand the purport of this jewel-like booklet. Thus he has defined who is qualified to relish this booklet.

ādadānas tṛṇaṁ dantair   idaṁ yāce punaḥ punaḥ
śrīmad rūpa padāmbhoja   rajo'haṁ syāṁ bhave bhave

ādadānaḥ - taking; *tṛṇaṁ* - a blade of grass; *dantaiḥ* - with the teeth; *idaṁ* - this; *yāce* - I pray; *punaḥ punaḥ* - again and again; *śrīmad rūpa* - Śrīla Rūpa Gosvāmī; *padāmbhoja* - lotusfeet; *rajaḥ* - dust; *aham* - I; *syāṁ* - may be; *bhave bhave* - birth after birth.

Taking a straw between my teeth I pray again and again that I may remain the dust of Śrīla Rūpa Gosvāmī's lotusfeet, birth after birth! (175)

Notes: *vividha rasa siddhānta sāgaraṁ pradarśya niṣpratyuha rasa-niṣpattau tathā rasa-rāji supariveṣaṇe cādvitīyāḥ śrīmad rūpa gosvāmīpādāḥ khalu gauḍīya vaiṣṇava mātrāṇām eva jīvātavaḥ — kim uta teṣāṁ tac caraṇāravindaika śaraṇānām śrī dāsa gosvāmi mahānubhāvānām iti jñeyam* — Revealing an ocean of different kinds of *rasa siddhāntas*, Śrīmad Rūpa Gosvāmīpāda is the most qualified person to dish out the quintessence of *rasa*, and he is the very life of all the Gauḍīya Vaiṣṇavas. What to speak of greatly realised souls like Śrī Dāsa Gosvāmī, who have taken exclusive shelter of his lotus feet?

prerito lalitā śaktyā mohāndha-matir apy ayam
mūla granthasya tātparya vyākhyāyāṁ labdha sāhasaḥ

tat pāda nalinī-dhūli kāruṇya leśa lubdhakaḥ
yad atra prālapaṁ mūḍhaḥ kṣamantāṁ te kṛpābdhayaḥ
vasu-bāṇamati śāke gaja-candra samanvite
navadvīpe nivasatā kenāpyalaṁ kṛto'nvayaḥ

Engaged by Lalitā-*sakhī*'s energy I have gained the courage to comment on the original book, although my intelligence is blinded by illusion. May these oceans of mercy forgive this fool, who is greedy for a little mercy from her lotusfeet, for speaking so much nonsense. Some worthless person who lives in Navadvīpa has made this commentary in the year 1858 Śāka-era (1937).

Thus ends Śrīla Raghunātha dāsa Gosvāmī's
Dāna keli Cintāmaṇiḥ.